I0012644

Mobile App Development with React Native

Create Cross-Platform Apps for iOS and Android with Ease

Greyson Chesterfield

COPYRIGHT

© [2024] by All rights reserved.

No part of this publication may be reproduced, distributed, or transmitted in any form or by any means, including photocopying, recording, or other electronic or mechanical methods, without the prior written permission of the publisher, except in the case of brief quotations embodied in critical reviews and certain other noncommercial uses permitted by copyright law.

DISCLAIMER

The information provided in this book is for general informational purposes only. All content in this book reflects the author's views and is based on their research, knowledge, and experiences. The author and publisher make no representations or warranties of any kind concerning the completeness, accuracy, reliability, suitability, or availability of the information contained herein.

This book is not intended to be a substitute for professional advice, diagnosis, or treatment. Readers should seek professional advice for any specific concerns or conditions. The author and publisher disclaim any liability or responsibility for any direct, indirect, incidental, or consequential loss or damage arising from the use of the information contained in this book.

Contents

Chapter 1: What is React Native?

Mobile app development has transformed how businesses, individuals, and industries interact with technology. But for developers, the choice of frameworks and tools can determine the efficiency, scalability, and success of their projects. React Native is one of the standout tools in this domain. In this chapter, we'll explore what React Native is, its history, why it has become a preferred choice for mobile app development, and the key features that make it a game-changer.

Overview of React Native and Its History

React Native Defined

React Native is a popular open-source framework for building mobile applications. Developed by Facebook, it allows developers to use JavaScript and React—a library primarily used for building web user interfaces—to create fully functional, cross-platform mobile applications. Apps built with React Native achieve a native-like performance while sharing a single codebase for both iOS and Android platforms.

Unlike traditional mobile development, which often requires separate codebases written in languages like

Swift/Objective-C for iOS and Java/Kotlin for Android, React Native bridges the gap, enabling efficient and unified development.

A Brief History

The story of React Native began in 2013 when a Facebook engineer, Jordan Walke, experimented with combining the React library with native UI elements. The idea was revolutionary: use React's declarative components to generate native UI elements instead of relying on web-based views. This led to the first public release of React Native in 2015.

React Native quickly gained traction among developers and businesses due to its ability to simplify mobile app development. Companies like Instagram, Airbnb, and Discord adopted the framework early on, showcasing its potential in real-world applications. Since its inception, React Native has evolved to become a robust and versatile framework with a thriving ecosystem and community.

Why Choose React Native for Mobile App Development?

Developers and businesses gravitate toward React Native for several reasons:

1. **Cross-Platform Development**
   Traditionally, creating an app for both iOS and Android involved maintaining two separate codebases. This doubled the workload, increased costs, and complicated updates. React Native allows

developers to write one codebase that works on both platforms, drastically reducing development time and effort.

For instance, if you're building a chat app, you don't need to write separate logic for rendering messages in Android and iOS—React Native handles it for you. This enables faster delivery of features and easier maintenance.

2. **Cost-Effectiveness**
   By sharing code across platforms, React Native reduces development costs. Businesses no longer need to hire separate teams for Android and iOS development, making it an excellent choice for startups and budget-conscious projects.

3. **Fast Development Cycles with Hot Reloading**
   One of React Native's standout features is **hot reloading**, which allows developers to see the results of their code changes in real-time without restarting the entire app. This boosts productivity, minimizes downtime, and makes debugging significantly easier.

Imagine tweaking the color of a button or adjusting the padding of a card. Instead of rebuilding and redeploying the app, you see the changes instantly, allowing for rapid iteration.

4. **Native Performance**
   Apps built with React Native perform comparably to fully native apps. Instead of relying on web views to render content (like frameworks such as Cordova or Ionic), React Native bridges JavaScript and native modules, enabling seamless communication and execution.

This means that users experience smooth animations, responsive UIs, and fast load times—essential qualities for a competitive mobile app.

5. **Large and Active Community**
   As an open-source project, React Native benefits from a massive community of developers who contribute plugins, tools, and solutions to common challenges. Whether you need a library for state management or help integrating a third-party API, chances are the React Native community has already created something that fits your needs.

6. **Ecosystem and Support**
   React Native is backed by Facebook, ensuring continuous updates and improvements. The framework integrates seamlessly with popular tools and libraries, such as Redux for state management, Axios for API calls, and Expo for quick prototyping. The extensive ecosystem makes React Native a complete solution for modern mobile app development.

Key Features and Benefits

1. Cross-Platform Compatibility

React Native's promise of "Learn Once, Write Anywhere" lies at its core. Developers can use the same JavaScript and React knowledge to build apps for iOS and Android. While minor adjustments are often needed for platform-specific features (e.g., differences in navigation styles), the bulk of the codebase remains shared.

Real-World Example:
A food delivery app might have slightly different layouts for Android and iOS users, such as the placement of navigation bars. With React Native, you can manage these variations while reusing most of the core logic, such as fetching restaurant data or handling user authentication.

2. Hot Reloading and Fast Iteration
Hot reloading is a feature that changes how developers interact with the codebase. By instantly applying changes without losing the app's current state, developers can test and tweak UI elements, debug logic, and experiment with functionality at lightning speed.

Developer Story:
Imagine building a weather app. You want to see how a new animation looks when transitioning between sunny and rainy weather themes. With hot reloading, you can adjust the animation parameters and instantly preview the results, saving hours of development time.

3. Native Performance
React Native leverages native modules and APIs, meaning the UI components are rendered using the native platform's capabilities. This ensures a smooth user experience that feels indistinguishable from fully native apps. Performance bottlenecks are rare, and developers can always write platform-specific native code if necessary.

Insight:
For apps that require heavy computations (e.g., gaming or AR apps), React Native provides flexibility by allowing the

critical parts to be implemented natively while maintaining the rest of the app in JavaScript.

4. Modular Architecture and Code Reusability
React Native promotes modular development, enabling teams to separate features into individual, reusable components. This modularity reduces redundancy and accelerates development. Teams working on large-scale projects often use this structure to manage complexity.

Example:
In an e-commerce app, components like "Product Card," "Search Bar," and "Checkout Form" can be reused across multiple screens, minimizing duplication and ensuring consistency.

5. Thriving Plugin Ecosystem
React Native has a rich library of third-party plugins and components, ranging from maps and charts to advanced animations. This ecosystem reduces the need to reinvent the wheel and accelerates app development.

Example:
A fitness tracking app can integrate GPS functionality with ease using the react-native-maps library, allowing users to view routes and track their exercise progress without developers building a custom mapping solution.

6. Seamless Integration with Native Code
For projects that require platform-specific capabilities, React Native allows developers to integrate native modules

written in Java, Swift, or Objective-C. This ensures that no functionality is out of reach.

Real-World Application:
An augmented reality (AR) app might use React Native for the general UI but rely on native libraries like ARKit or ARCore for the AR experience.

7. Growing Adoption by Industry Leaders

React Native's credibility is cemented by its use in apps built by leading companies. Apps like Instagram, Skype, Airbnb (earlier versions), and Bloomberg highlight its versatility across industries.

Case Study:
The Facebook Ads Manager app was developed using React Native, demonstrating its ability to handle complex interfaces and high-performance requirements.

Chapter 2: Setting Up Your Development Environment

Before diving into building apps with React Native, you must first set up a reliable development environment. This chapter provides a step-by-step guide to configuring your system for React Native development on Windows, macOS, and Linux. By the end, you'll have everything you need to create, run, and debug your React Native applications.

Why Setting Up Your Environment Properly is Crucial

React Native requires a mix of tools that work together seamlessly, including Node.js, package managers (npm or yarn), an emulator or simulator for testing, and platform-specific tools like Android Studio and Xcode. A properly configured environment ensures smooth development, faster debugging, and reliable testing for both iOS and Android.

Step-by-Step Guide for Setting Up React Native

Let's break the setup process into three key steps:

1. **Installing Core Dependencies**

    o Node.js and npm/yarn

    o Expo CLI or React Native CLI

2. **Configuring Platform-Specific Tools**

    o Android Studio for Android

    o Xcode for iOS (macOS only)

3. **Testing Your Installation**

---

1. Installing Core Dependencies

1.1 Installing Node.js and npm/yarn

React Native relies on **Node.js**, a JavaScript runtime, and its associated package manager **npm** (Node Package Manager) or **yarn**.

Steps to Install Node.js:

1. Visit the Node.js official website.

2. Download the **LTS (Long-Term Support)** version, which is stable and suitable for most projects.

3. Follow the installation instructions for your operating system.

    o For macOS: Use the installer package or install via Homebrew:

bash

brew install node

> o For Linux: Use your package manager (e.g.,
>   apt, yum) or Node Version Manager (NVM)
>   for flexibility.

bash

```
curl -o- https://raw.githubusercontent.com/nvm-
sh/nvm/v0.39.0/install.sh | bash
```

nvm install --lts

> o For Windows: Run the downloaded .msi
>   installer.

4. Verify the installation:

bash

node -v

npm -v

Optional: Installing Yarn
Yarn is an alternative to npm that some developers prefer
for faster dependency management.
Install yarn globally:

bash

npm install -g yarn

1.2 Installing Expo CLI or React Native CLI

React Native supports two primary workflows: **Expo CLI** and **React Native CLI**. Choose one based on your needs:

Expo CLI:
Expo is an all-in-one development platform that simplifies React Native app development, especially for beginners. It abstracts platform-specific setup and provides additional tools for rapid prototyping.

To install Expo CLI globally:

bash

```
npm install -g expo-cli
```

Create a new Expo project:

bash

```
expo init MyFirstApp
cd MyFirstApp
expo start
```

React Native CLI:
For full control over the native side of your app, use React Native CLI. This workflow requires additional setup for Android Studio and Xcode.

Install React Native CLI globally:

bash

```
npm install -g react-native-cli
```

Create a new project:

bash

npx react-native init MyFirstApp

---

2. Configuring Platform-Specific Tools

2.1 Setting Up Android Studio (Required for Android Development)

To build and test Android apps, you need to install Android Studio, which includes the Android SDK, emulators, and other essential tools.

Steps to Install and Configure Android Studio:

1. Download Android Studio from the official website.

2. Run the installer and follow the prompts to complete the installation.

3. Configure Android Studio:

   o Open Android Studio.

   o Go to **Preferences (macOS)** or **File > Settings (Windows/Linux)**.

   o Navigate to **Appearance & Behavior > System Settings > Android SDK**.

- Ensure the following items are checked and installed:

    - **Android SDK Platform-Tools**

    - **Android SDK Build-Tools**

    - **Android Emulator**

    - The latest Android API level (e.g., API Level 31 or higher).

4. Set up an Android Virtual Device (AVD):

    - Go to **Tools > AVD Manager**.

    - Click **Create Virtual Device** and select a device (e.g., Pixel 5).

    - Choose a system image (e.g., Android 12) and finish the setup.

5. Add the Android SDK to your system's PATH environment variable:

    - **Windows:**

        - Locate the SDK folder (e.g., C:\Users\<YourUsername>\AppData\Local\Android\Sdk).

        - Add this path to your system's PATH variable.

    - **macOS/Linux:**
      Add the following lines to your ~/.bashrc or ~/.zshrc file:

bash

export ANDROID_HOME=$HOME/Library/Android/sdk

export
PATH=$ANDROID_HOME/emulator:$ANDROID_HOM
E/tools:$ANDROID_HOME/tools/bin:$ANDROID_HOM
E/platform-tools:$PATH

- o Run source ~/.bashrc or source ~/.zshrc to apply changes.

6. Test your setup:
   Start an emulator from Android Studio or run the following command:

bash

emulator -list-avds

emulator -avd <Your_AVD_Name>

2.2 Setting Up Xcode (Required for iOS Development, macOS Only)

To develop iOS apps, you need **Xcode**, which includes tools like the iOS simulator and developer utilities.

Steps to Install and Configure Xcode:

1. Download Xcode from the Mac App Store or Apple's developer website.

2. Install Xcode Command Line Tools:
   Open Terminal and run:

bash

```
xcode-select --install
```

3. Open Xcode and accept the license agreement.

4. Configure Xcode:

   o Go to **Xcode > Preferences > Locations**.

   o Set the Command Line Tools dropdown to the latest Xcode version.

5. Verify installation:
   Run the following commands to ensure Xcode and the tools are accessible:

bash

```
xcodebuild -version
```

6. Test the iOS Simulator:

   o Open Xcode.

   o Go to **Xcode > Open Developer Tool > Simulator**.

   o Choose a device (e.g., iPhone 14) to simulate.

Note: Apple requires a developer account to run apps on physical iOS devices. A free account works for testing, but a paid account is needed for publishing apps.

3. Testing Your Installation

To ensure everything is configured correctly, test your setup by running a basic React Native app.

Testing with Expo CLI

1. Navigate to your Expo project folder:

bash

cd MyFirstApp

2. Start the development server:

bash

expo start

3. Scan the QR code displayed in the terminal or browser using the Expo Go app (available on iOS and Android). The app should load on your device or emulator.

Testing with React Native CLI

1. Navigate to your React Native project folder:

bash

cd MyFirstApp

2. Run the app on an Android emulator:

bash

```
npx react-native run-android
```

3. Run the app on an iOS simulator (macOS only):

bash

```
npx react-native run-ios
```

Troubleshooting:

- If you encounter errors, verify that the Android SDK, emulator, and Xcode tools are correctly configured.

- Check environment variables and ensure dependencies are up-to-date.

Chapter 3:
Understanding the
Basics of React Native

Before diving into building complex apps with React
Native, it's essential to understand the foundational
concepts that make the framework powerful and versatile.
This chapter explores the core principles of JavaScript and
React that you need to know, explains how React Native's
architecture bridges JavaScript with native platforms, and
introduces the key components you'll use to create
interfaces.

JavaScript and React: What You Need to Know

React Native is built on two fundamental technologies:
JavaScript and **React**. Let's break down their roles and the
key concepts you should grasp to work effectively with
React Native.

JavaScript: The Backbone of React Native

JavaScript is a versatile, high-level programming language
primarily used for web development. In React Native,
JavaScript enables developers to write the logic and
behavior of mobile applications.

Key JavaScript Concepts for React Native:

1. **Variables and Data Types**
   Use let and const to declare variables. React Native frequently handles objects, arrays, and functions.

javascript

```
const name = "React Native";
let counter = 0;
```

2. **Functions and Arrow Functions**
   Functions are central to React Native for handling events and managing logic. Arrow functions (() => {}) are a common shorthand in modern JavaScript.

javascript

```
const greet = (name) => `Hello, ${name}!`;
```

3. **Modules and Imports**
   React Native components and libraries are organized into modules, which you import as needed.

javascript

```
import React from 'react';
import { View, Text } from 'react-native';
```

4. **Promises and Async/Await**
   Asynchronous operations like API calls rely on
   promises.

javascript

```javascript
const fetchData = async () => {

  const response = await
fetch('https://api.example.com/data');

  const data = await response.json();

  console.log(data);

};
```

5. **ES6+ Syntax**
   Modern JavaScript (ES6+) introduces features like
   destructuring, template literals, and the spread/rest
   operators, which are widely used in React Native.

javascript

```javascript
const { name, age } = user;  // Destructuring

const greeting = `Hello, ${name}!`;  // Template literals

const updatedList = [...list, newItem];  // Spread operator
```

React: The Foundation of React Native

React is a library for building user interfaces. React Native
extends React's capabilities to mobile app development.

Key React Concepts for React Native:

1. **Components**
   React Native apps are built using components, which are reusable UI elements.

javascript

```javascript
const MyComponent = () => {
  return (
    <View>
      <Text>Hello, world!</Text>
    </View>
  );
};
```

2. **State and Props**
   - **State** manages dynamic data within a component.
   - **Props** pass data between components.

javascript

```javascript
const Counter = () => {
  const [count, setCount] = React.useState(0);
  return (
    <View>
      <Text>{count}</Text>
```

```
      <Button title="Increase" onPress={() =>
setCount(count + 1)} />

    </View>

  );

};
```

3. **Hooks**
   Hooks like useState and useEffect simplify
   managing state and lifecycle methods in functional
   components.

javascript

```
React.useEffect(() => {

  console.log('Component mounted');

}, []);
```

4. **JSX**
   JSX allows you to write HTML-like syntax in
   JavaScript, making UI creation intuitive.

javascript

```
const App = () => (

  <View>

    <Text>Hello, JSX!</Text>

  </View>

);
```

The React Native Architecture: Native Modules and the JavaScript Thread

React Native bridges the gap between JavaScript and native mobile platforms through its architecture. Understanding this bridge is crucial for optimizing performance and leveraging React Native's strengths.

How React Native Works

1. **JavaScript Thread**
   The JavaScript thread handles the business logic, application state, and interactions with the user. This is where most of your code runs.

2. **Bridge**
   React Native uses a bridge to communicate between JavaScript and native code. For example, when a user presses a button, the action is sent to the JavaScript thread via the bridge, and any updates are rendered on the screen.

3. **Native Modules**
   Native modules are written in platform-specific languages (Java/Kotlin for Android, Swift/Objective-C for iOS) and provide access to device features like the camera or GPS. React Native provides built-in modules, and you can create custom modules if needed.

Optimizing Performance

Understanding the separation of concerns between the JavaScript thread and native modules helps in avoiding bottlenecks. For example:

- Minimize heavy computations on the JavaScript thread.

- Use native modules for performance-intensive tasks.

Key Components in React Native

React Native provides a set of core components to build mobile user interfaces. Let's explore the most commonly used ones:

1. View

The View component is the basic building block of React Native's UI, equivalent to a <div> in web development. It acts as a container for other components.

Example:

javascript

```
import { View } from 'react-native';


const App = () => {
  return (
```

```
    <View style={{ padding: 10, backgroundColor:
'lightgray' }}>

        <Text>Hello, View!</Text>

    </View>

  );

};
```

Common Use Cases:

- Layouts

- Wrapping multiple child components

2. Text

The Text component is used to display textual content.
Unlike in web development, you must use Text for all text
in React Native.

Example:

javascript

```
import { Text } from 'react-native';


const App = () => {
```

```
  return (

    <Text style={{ fontSize: 18, color: 'blue' }}>

      Welcome to React Native!

    </Text>

  );

};
```

Key Features:

- Supports nested text styles.
- Handles touchable text with onPress.

3. Image

The Image component is used to display images. It supports remote URLs, local assets, and SVG files.

Example:

javascript

```
import { Image } from 'react-native';


const App = () => {

  return (
```

```
  <Image
    source={{ uri: 'https://example.com/image.jpg' }}
    style={{ width: 100, height: 100 }}
  />
  );
};
```

Key Features:

- Supports resizing and scaling.
- Handles placeholders and loading indicators.

4. ScrollView

The ScrollView component enables scrolling for content that exceeds the screen size.

Example:

javascript

```
import { ScrollView, Text } from 'react-native';


const App = () => {
  return (
    <ScrollView style={{ padding: 10 }}>
```

```
{Array.from({ length: 50 }, (_, i) => (
    <Text key={i}>Item {i + 1}</Text>
))}
        </ScrollView>
    );
};
```

Key Features:

- Horizontal and vertical scrolling.
- Built-in support for touch gestures.

5. StyleSheet

React Native uses StyleSheet to define styles for components. While you can use inline styles, StyleSheet provides better organization and performance.

Example:

javascript

```
import { StyleSheet, Text, View } from 'react-native';

const App = () => {
    return (
        <View style={styles.container}>
```

```
      <Text style={styles.text}>Styled with
StyleSheet</Text>

    </View>

  );
};


const styles = StyleSheet.create({
  container: {
    flex: 1,
    justifyContent: 'center',
    alignItems: 'center',
    backgroundColor: 'lightblue',
  },
  text: {
    fontSize: 20,
    color: 'white',
  },
});
```

Advantages:

- Provides validation for styles.
- Optimized for performance.

Chapter 4: Creating Your First App

Building your first app in React Native is an exciting milestone! In this chapter, we'll guide you through creating a simple "To-Do List" app—a project that introduces essential concepts like user input, state management, and rendering lists. We'll use Expo for quick prototyping, debug common issues, and test the app to ensure it works as intended.

Project Overview: The To-Do List App

The To-Do List app allows users to:

1. Add tasks to a list.

2. View a list of tasks.

3. Remove tasks from the list.

This beginner-friendly project will teach you:

- Using React Native components like TextInput, Button, and FlatList.

- Managing state with useState.

- Styling components with StyleSheet.

- Debugging and testing the app.

Setting Up Your Environment with Expo

Expo simplifies the development process by providing pre-configured tools for building and testing React Native apps. If you haven't set up Expo yet, follow these steps:

1. Install Expo CLI globally:

bash

```
npm install -g expo-cli
```

2. Create a new project:

bash

```
expo init ToDoApp
cd ToDoApp
```

3. Start the development server:

bash

```
expo start
```

4. Scan the QR code in the terminal using the Expo Go app (available for iOS and Android) or run the app on an emulator/simulator.

Step 1: Structuring the To-Do List App

The app will have three main parts:

1. **Input Area**: A TextInput and Button for adding tasks.

2. **Task List**: A scrollable list (FlatList) to display tasks.

3. **Delete Functionality**: Allow users to remove tasks.

Here's an outline of the code structure:

javascript

```
import React, { useState } from 'react';
import { View, Text, TextInput, Button, FlatList,
StyleSheet, TouchableOpacity } from 'react-native';


export default function App() {
  const [task, setTask] = useState('');
  const [tasks, setTasks] = useState([]);


  const addTask = () => {
    // Add task logic
  };
```

```
const removeTask = (id) => {
  // Remove task logic
};


return (
  <View style={styles.container}>
    {/* Input Area */}
    <View style={styles.inputArea}>
      <TextInput
        placeholder="Enter a task"
        style={styles.input}
        value={task}
        onChangeText={(text) => setTask(text)}
      />
      <Button title="Add" onPress={addTask} />
    </View>

    {/* Task List */}
    <FlatList
      data={tasks}
      keyExtractor={(item) => item.id}
      renderItem={({ item }) => (
```

```jsx
        <TouchableOpacity onPress={() =>
removeTask(item.id)}>

          <Text style={styles.task}>{item.text}</Text>

          </TouchableOpacity>

      )}
      />

    </View>

  );
}


const styles = StyleSheet.create({

  // Styles go here

});
```

Step 2: Adding Functionality

Adding Tasks

We'll use useState to manage the task being entered (task) and the list of tasks (tasks).

1. **Updating the State for Tasks**
   Modify the addTask function to add a new task:

javascript

```javascript
const addTask = () => {
    if (task.trim().length === 0) return; // Ignore empty tasks
    const newTask = { id: Date.now().toString(), text: task };
    setTasks([...tasks, newTask]);
    setTask(''); // Clear the input
};
```

2. **Connecting the Input to the State**
   The TextInput updates the task state whenever the user types:

javascript

```javascript
<TextInput
    placeholder="Enter a task"
    style={styles.input}
    value={task}
    onChangeText={(text) => setTask(text)}
/>
```

Displaying Tasks

We'll use a FlatList to render the list of tasks. It's efficient and optimized for scrolling.

1. **Rendering the Task List**
   Each task will be displayed as a touchable text element:

javascript

```
<FlatList

  data={tasks}

  keyExtractor={(item) => item.id}

  renderItem={({ item }) => (

    <TouchableOpacity onPress={() =>
removeTask(item.id)}>

        <Text style={styles.task}>{item.text}</Text>

    </TouchableOpacity>

  )}
/>
```

2. **Why Use FlatList?**
   FlatList improves performance by rendering only visible items, making it ideal for long lists.

Removing Tasks

The removeTask function filters out the task with the matching id:

javascript

```javascript
const removeTask = (id) => {

    setTasks(tasks.filter((task) => task.id !== id));

};
```

Each task becomes a touchable element. When tapped, it triggers the removeTask function.

Step 3: Styling the App

We'll use StyleSheet to define styles for the components.

javascript

```javascript
const styles = StyleSheet.create({
    container: {
        flex: 1,
        padding: 20,
        backgroundColor: '#f8f8f8',
    },
    inputArea: {
        flexDirection: 'row',
        marginBottom: 20,
    },
    input: {
```

```
    flex: 1,

    borderWidth: 1,

    borderColor: '#ccc',

    padding: 10,

    borderRadius: 5,

    marginRight: 10,

  },

  task: {

    backgroundColor: '#e0e0e0',

    padding: 15,

    borderRadius: 5,

    marginBottom: 10,

  },

});
```

Step 4: Debugging and Testing the App

Debugging Common Issues

1. **Debugging in Expo**

   - o   Use the console in your browser or terminal
     for error messages.

- o Open the Expo Developer Tools (automatically starts with expo start) to monitor logs.

2. **React Native Debugger**
   Use React Developer Tools to inspect the component tree and state. Install it globally:

bash

```
npm install -g react-devtools
```

3. **Common Errors**
   - o **Empty Task Error**: Ensure the addTask function checks for empty input:

javascript

```
if (task.trim().length === 0) return;
```

   - o **Unique Key Error**: Each item in FlatList requires a unique keyExtractor:

javascript

```
keyExtractor={(item) => item.id}
```

Testing the App

1. **Manual Testing**
   - o Add tasks and verify they appear in the list.

o Tap on a task to ensure it's removed.

o Test edge cases like entering empty tasks or rapid additions/removals.

2. **Testing on Physical Devices**

o Run the app on your device using Expo Go.

o Ensure the UI scales properly across different screen sizes.

3. **Automated Testing**
Write basic unit tests using Jest to verify core functionality:

javascript

```javascript
test('adds a task to the list', () => {
  const [tasks, setTasks] = React.useState([]);
  const addTask = (task) => setTasks([...tasks, { id: '1', text: task }]);

  addTask('New Task');
  expect(tasks.length).toBe(1);
  expect(tasks[0].text).toBe('New Task');
});
```

Final App Code

Here's the completed app:

javascript

```javascript
import React, { useState } from 'react';
import { View, Text, TextInput, Button, FlatList,
StyleSheet, TouchableOpacity } from 'react-native';

export default function App() {
  const [task, setTask] = useState('');
  const [tasks, setTasks] = useState([]);

  const addTask = () => {
    if (task.trim().length === 0) return;
    const newTask = { id: Date.now().toString(), text: task
};
    setTasks([...tasks, newTask]);
    setTask('');
  };

  const removeTask = (id) => {
    setTasks(tasks.filter((task) => task.id !== id));
```

```jsx
  };

  return (
    <View style={styles.container}>
      <View style={styles.inputArea}>
        <TextInput
          placeholder="Enter a task"
          style={styles.input}
          value={task}
          onChangeText={(text) => setTask(text)}
        />
        <Button title="Add" onPress={addTask} />
      </View>
      <FlatList
        data={tasks}
        keyExtractor={(item) => item.id}
        renderItem={({ item }) => (
          <TouchableOpacity onPress={() =>
removeTask(item.id)}>
            <Text style={styles.task}>{item.text}</Text>
          </TouchableOpacity>
        )}
```

```
        />
      </View>
    );
  }


const styles = StyleSheet.create({
  container: {
    flex: 1,
    padding: 20,
    backgroundColor: '#f8f8f8',
  },
  inputArea: {
    flexDirection: 'row',
    marginBottom: 20,
  },
  input: {
    flex: 1,
    borderWidth: 1,
    borderColor: '#ccc',
    padding: 10,
    borderRadius: 5,
    marginRight: 10,
```

```
  },
  task: {
    backgroundColor: '#e0e0e0',
    padding: 15,
    borderRadius: 5,
    marginBottom: 10,
  },
});
```

Chapter 5: Navigation in React Native

Navigation is a critical component of any mobile app, allowing users to seamlessly move between different screens. React Native provides several options for implementing navigation, but the most popular and versatile library is **React Navigation**. In this chapter, we'll cover how to use React Navigation for common patterns like **Stack**, **Tab**, and **Drawer navigation**. We'll also explore advanced topics like handling **deep linking** and **passing data between screens**.

Introduction to React Navigation

React Navigation is a powerful library designed specifically for React Native apps. It supports:

- **Stack Navigation**: Sequential navigation with a back button (e.g., navigating between pages in a form).

- **Tab Navigation**: Horizontal tabs at the bottom or top of the screen (e.g., switching between feeds, messages, and profile in a social app).

- **Drawer Navigation**: A side menu that slides out (e.g., accessing app settings or user profile).

To get started, install the library:

bash

```
npm install @react-navigation/native react-native-screens
react-native-safe-area-context react-native-gesture-handler
react-native-reanimated react-native-vector-icons @react-native-masked-view/masked-view
```

```
npm install @react-navigation/stack
```

For Tab or Drawer navigation, install additional dependencies:

bash

```
npm install @react-navigation/bottom-tabs
```

```
npm install @react-navigation/drawer
```

Ensure that your project is properly configured to support React Navigation by wrapping the app in NavigationContainer.

---

1. Stack Navigation

Overview

Stack navigation mimics the behavior of a call stack, where screens are pushed and popped as users navigate. It's ideal for workflows like onboarding or hierarchical navigation.

Implementation

1. **Setup Stack Navigator**

```javascript
import React from 'react';
import { View, Text, Button } from 'react-native';
import { createStackNavigator } from '@react-navigation/stack';
import { NavigationContainer } from '@react-navigation/native';

const Stack = createStackNavigator();

const HomeScreen = ({ navigation }) => (
  <View>
    <Text>Home Screen</Text>
    <Button
      title="Go to Details"
      onPress={() => navigation.navigate('Details', { itemId: 42 })}
    />
  </View>
);

const DetailsScreen = ({ route }) => {
```

```
const { itemId } = route.params;
return (
  <View>
    <Text>Details Screen</Text>
    <Text>Item ID: {itemId}</Text>
  </View>
);
};


export default function App() {
  return (
    <NavigationContainer>
      <Stack.Navigator>
        <Stack.Screen name="Home"
component={HomeScreen} />
        <Stack.Screen name="Details"
component={DetailsScreen} />
      </Stack.Navigator>
    </NavigationContainer>
  );
}
```

2. **Passing Data Between Screens**

- o Pass data using the navigate function's second argument:

javascript

```
navigation.navigate('Details', { itemId: 42 });
```

- o Access the passed data in the target screen using route.params:

javascript

```
const { itemId } = route.params;
```

3. **Customizing the Header** Customize headers for individual screens:

javascript

```
<Stack.Screen
    name="Details"
    component={DetailsScreen}
    options={{ title: 'Custom Title' }}
/>
```

---

2. Tab Navigation

Overview

Tab navigation allows users to switch between multiple screens using tabs, typically placed at the bottom of the screen.

Implementation

1. **Setup Tab Navigator**

javascript

```
import React from 'react';

import { View, Text } from 'react-native';

import { createBottomTabNavigator } from '@react-navigation/bottom-tabs';

import { NavigationContainer } from '@react-navigation/native';


const Tab = createBottomTabNavigator();


const HomeScreen = () => (
  <View>
    <Text>Home Screen</Text>
  </View>
);


const ProfileScreen = () => (
```

```jsx
    <View>

      <Text>Profile Screen</Text>

    </View>

  );



export default function App() {

  return (

    <NavigationContainer>

      <Tab.Navigator>

        <Tab.Screen name="Home"
component={HomeScreen} />

        <Tab.Screen name="Profile"
component={ProfileScreen} />

      </Tab.Navigator>

    </NavigationContainer>

  );

}
```

2. **Customizing Tab Icons** Use the options prop to customize icons for each tab:

javascript

```jsx
<Tab.Screen

  name="Home"
```

```
        component={HomeScreen}

        options={{

          tabBarIcon: ({ color, size }) => (

            <Ionicons name="home" size={size} color={color}
/>

          ),

        }}
/>
```

3. **Styling the Tab Bar** Customize the tab bar using
    the tabBarOptions prop:

javascript

```
<Tab.Navigator

    screenOptions={{

      tabBarStyle: { backgroundColor: 'black' },

      tabBarActiveTintColor: 'white',

      tabBarInactiveTintColor: 'gray',

    }}
>
```

3. Drawer Navigation

Overview

Drawer navigation provides a hidden side menu that users can access by swiping or tapping a menu icon.

Implementation

1. **Setup Drawer Navigator**

javascript

```
import React from 'react';

import { View, Text } from 'react-native';

import { createDrawerNavigator } from '@react-navigation/drawer';

import { NavigationContainer } from '@react-navigation/native';


const Drawer = createDrawerNavigator();


const HomeScreen = () => (
  <View>
    <Text>Home Screen</Text>
  </View>
);


const SettingsScreen = () => (
  <View>
```

```
    <Text>Settings Screen</Text>
  </View>
);


export default function App() {
  return (
    <NavigationContainer>
      <Drawer.Navigator>
        <Drawer.Screen name="Home"
component={HomeScreen} />
        <Drawer.Screen name="Settings"
component={SettingsScreen} />
      </Drawer.Navigator>
    </NavigationContainer>
  );
}
```

2. **Customizing Drawer Content** Replace the default drawer with a custom design:

javascript

```
<Drawer.Navigator
  drawerContent={(props) => (
    <CustomDrawerContent {...props} />
```

```javascript
    )}
/>
```

Example of a custom drawer:

javascript

```javascript
const CustomDrawerContent = (props) => (
  <DrawerContentScrollView {...props}>
    <DrawerItem
      label="Home"
      onPress={() => props.navigation.navigate('Home')}
    />
    <DrawerItem
      label="Settings"
      onPress={() =>
props.navigation.navigate('Settings')}
    />
  </DrawerContentScrollView>
);
```

4. Handling Deep Linking

Deep linking allows users to navigate directly to specific screens in your app via URLs. This is particularly useful for opening apps from emails, notifications, or other apps.

Setting Up Deep Linking

1. **Configure NavigationContainer** Add a linking configuration to the NavigationContainer:

javascript

```javascript
const linking = {

  prefixes: ['https://example.com', 'example://'],

  config: {

    screens: {

      Home: '',

      Details: 'details/:itemId',

    },

  },

};


export default function App() {

  return (

    <NavigationContainer linking={linking}>
```

```
<Stack.Navigator>

    <Stack.Screen name="Home"
component={HomeScreen} />

    <Stack.Screen name="Details"
component={DetailsScreen} />

  </Stack.Navigator>

 </NavigationContainer>

 );

}
```

2. **Handle Dynamic Links** The route.params object will automatically populate with dynamic parameters like itemId from the URL:

   o   URL: example://details/42

   o   Access in DetailsScreen:

javascript

```
const { itemId } = route.params;
```

---

5. Passing Data Between Screens

Passing Data with Navigation

Data is typically passed between screens using the navigate function:

javascript

```javascript
navigation.navigate('Details', { itemId: 42 });
```

Fetching Data on Target Screens

The target screen can fetch the data from route.params:

javascript

```javascript
const { itemId } = route.params;
```

Using Context for Global Data

For more complex apps, consider using React Context or state management libraries like Redux to share data globally across screens.

Chapter 6: Styling in React Native

Styling plays a critical role in creating visually appealing and user-friendly mobile applications. React Native offers flexible styling options, responsive design techniques, and tools for implementing modern UI features like themes and dark mode. This chapter explores the differences between StyleSheet and inline styles, responsive design techniques like Flexbox and Dimensions, and advanced concepts like platform-specific styling and themes.

---

1. StyleSheet vs Inline Styles

React Native provides two main methods for styling components: **StyleSheet** and **inline styles**.

1.1 Using Inline Styles

Inline styles are applied directly to components via the style prop. They are defined as JavaScript objects.

Example:

javascript

```
import React from 'react';

import { View, Text } from 'react-native';
```

```
const App = () => {

    return (

        <View style={{ backgroundColor: 'blue', padding: 20
}}>

            <Text style={{ color: 'white', fontSize: 18
}}>Hello, World!</Text>

        </View>

    );

};
```

Advantages:

- Quick and convenient for small components.

- Easy to implement for dynamic styling (e.g., based on props or state).

Disadvantages:

- Not reusable; each component needs its own style definition.

- Less readable and maintainable for large projects.

1.2 Using StyleSheet

The StyleSheet API lets you define styles as JavaScript objects and reuse them across components. This improves readability and performance.

Example:

javascript

```javascript
import React from 'react';
import { View, Text, StyleSheet } from 'react-native';

const App = () => {
  return (
    <View style={styles.container}>
      <Text style={styles.text}>Hello, World!</Text>
    </View>
  );
};

const styles = StyleSheet.create({
  container: {
    backgroundColor: 'blue',
    padding: 20,
  },
  text: {
    color: 'white',
    fontSize: 18,
```

```
  },
});
```

Advantages:

- Reusable and maintainable styles.

- Validates styles at runtime for common mistakes.

- Optimized for performance by reducing re-renders.

Disadvantages:

- Slightly more verbose for simple styles.

When to Use Inline Styles vs StyleSheet

- Use **inline styles** for quick prototypes or dynamic styling based on component state or props.

- Use **StyleSheet** for reusable, scalable, and maintainable styles in larger projects.

---

2. Responsive Design Techniques

Mobile apps must adapt to various screen sizes, orientations, and platforms. React Native provides tools to build responsive designs efficiently.

2.1 Flexbox for Layout

Flexbox is the default layout model in React Native. It allows you to create flexible and adaptive layouts.

Key Properties:

- flexDirection: Defines the main axis (row or column). Default is column.

- justifyContent: Aligns children along the main axis.

- alignItems: Aligns children along the cross axis.

- flex: Allocates space to children.

Example:

javascript

```
import React from 'react';
import { View, Text, StyleSheet } from 'react-native';


const App = () => {
  return (
    <View style={styles.container}>
      <View style={styles.box}><Text>1</Text></View>
      <View style={styles.box}><Text>2</Text></View>
      <View style={styles.box}><Text>3</Text></View>
    </View>
  );
};
```

```javascript
const styles = StyleSheet.create({
  container: {
    flex: 1,
    flexDirection: 'row',
    justifyContent: 'space-around',
    alignItems: 'center',
  },
  box: {
    width: 50,
    height: 50,
    backgroundColor: 'lightblue',
    justifyContent: 'center',
    alignItems: 'center',
  },
});
```

2.2 Dimensions and Percentages

Use the Dimensions API to get the screen width and height dynamically, ensuring your app adjusts to different devices.

Example:

javascript

```jsx
import React from 'react';

import { View, Text, StyleSheet, Dimensions } from 'react-native';


const { width, height } = Dimensions.get('window');


const App = () => {
  return (
    <View style={[styles.container, { width: width * 0.8 }]}>
      <Text>Responsive Box</Text>
    </View>
  );
};


const styles = StyleSheet.create({
  container: {
    height: height * 0.2,
    backgroundColor: 'lightblue',
    justifyContent: 'center',
    alignItems: 'center',
  },
```

```
});
```

2.3 Platform-Specific Styling

React Native lets you apply platform-specific styles using
the Platform module or conditional logic.

Using the Platform Module:

javascript

```javascript
import { Platform, StyleSheet } from 'react-native';


const styles = StyleSheet.create({
    text: {
        fontSize: Platform.OS === 'ios' ? 20 : 18,
        color: Platform.OS === 'android' ? 'green' : 'blue',
    },
});
```

Using Conditional Logic:

javascript

```javascript
const containerStyle = {
    padding: Platform.OS === 'ios' ? 10 : 15,
    backgroundColor: Platform.OS === 'android' ? 'white' :
'gray',
```

```
};
```

2.4 Orientation Handling

Use the useWindowDimensions hook to handle orientation changes dynamically.

Example:

javascript

```
import React from 'react';
import { View, Text, StyleSheet, useWindowDimensions }
from 'react-native';


const App = () => {
  const { width, height } = useWindowDimensions();


  return (
    <View style={[styles.container, { flexDirection: width
> height ? 'row' : 'column' }]}>
      <Text>Responsive Layout</Text>
    </View>
  );
};
```

```javascript
const styles = StyleSheet.create({
  container: {
    flex: 1,
    justifyContent: 'center',
    alignItems: 'center',
  },
});
```

---

3. Themes and Dark Mode

Themes and dark mode enhance user experience by adapting the app's appearance to the user's preferences or system settings.

3.1 Implementing Themes

Themes are collections of styles that can be toggled dynamically.

Example:

javascript

```javascript
const lightTheme = {
  backgroundColor: 'white',
  textColor: 'black',
};
```

```javascript
const darkTheme = {

  backgroundColor: 'black',

  textColor: 'white',

};
```

Use useState or a context provider to manage the active theme.

Example:

javascript


```javascript
import React, { useState } from 'react';

import { View, Text, Button, StyleSheet } from 'react-native';


const App = () => {

  const [theme, setTheme] = useState(lightTheme);


  const toggleTheme = () => {

    setTheme((prevTheme) => (prevTheme === lightTheme ? darkTheme : lightTheme));

  };
```

```
  return (
    <View style={[styles.container, { backgroundColor:
theme.backgroundColor }]}>
      <Text style={{ color: theme.textColor }}>Dynamic
Theme</Text>
      <Button title="Toggle Theme"
onPress={toggleTheme} />
    </View>
  );
};


const lightTheme = {
  backgroundColor: 'white',
  textColor: 'black',
};


const darkTheme = {
  backgroundColor: 'black',
  textColor: 'white',
};


const styles = StyleSheet.create({
  container: {
```

```
    flex: 1,

    justifyContent: 'center',

    alignItems: 'center',

  },

});
```

3.2 Enabling Dark Mode

React Native's Appearance API detects the system theme (light or dark).

Example:

javascript

```
import React, { useState, useEffect } from 'react';

import { View, Text, StyleSheet, Appearance } from 'react-native';


const App = () => {

  const [theme, setTheme] =
useState(Appearance.getColorScheme());


  useEffect(() => {

    const listener = Appearance.addChangeListener(({
colorScheme }) => {
```

```
      setTheme(colorScheme);
    });
    return () => listener.remove();
  }, []);


  const backgroundColor = theme === 'dark' ? 'black' :
'white';
  const textColor = theme === 'dark' ? 'white' : 'black';


  return (
    <View style={[styles.container, { backgroundColor
}]}>
      <Text style={{ color: textColor }}>System Theme:
{theme}</Text>
    </View>
  );
};


const styles = StyleSheet.create({
  container: {
    flex: 1,
    justifyContent: 'center',
    alignItems: 'center',
```

```
  },
});
```

Chapter 7: State Management

State management is one of the most crucial aspects of building robust and scalable applications. In this chapter, we'll explore how to handle **local state** using useState and useReducer, manage **global state** with the Context API, and introduce advanced tools like **Redux** and alternatives such as Zustand.

---

1. What is State Management?

State management refers to how your application keeps track of data that changes over time. In React Native, state determines how components render and behave. For example:

- The text entered in an input field.

- Whether a modal is open or closed.

- The list of items displayed in a shopping cart.

State can be categorized as:

- **Local State**: State that is specific to a single component.

- **Global State**: State shared across multiple components or screens.

2. Local State Management

2.1 Managing Local State with useState

The useState hook is a simple and effective way to manage state in functional components. It allows you to create and update state variables.

Example: Counter Component

javascript

```javascript
import React, { useState } from 'react';
import { View, Text, Button, StyleSheet } from 'react-native';


const Counter = () => {
    const [count, setCount] = useState(0);


    return (
        <View style={styles.container}>
            <Text style={styles.text}>Count: {count}</Text>
            <Button title="Increase" onPress={() =>
setCount(count + 1)} />
            <Button title="Decrease" onPress={() =>
setCount(count - 1)} />
```

```jsx
      </View>
  );
};


const styles = StyleSheet.create({
  container: {
    flex: 1,
    justifyContent: 'center',
    alignItems: 'center',
  },
  text: {
    fontSize: 24,
    marginBottom: 20,
  },
});


export default Counter;
```

Advantages:

- Simple and straightforward.
- Ideal for managing UI-focused state, like toggles or form inputs.

Limitations:

- Not suitable for complex state logic or shared state.

2.2 Managing Complex State with useReducer

When state logic becomes complex, involving multiple related variables or intricate updates, useReducer is a better choice. It's especially useful for scenarios like managing form inputs or lists.

Example: To-Do List

javascript

```javascript
import React, { useReducer } from 'react';
import { View, Text, TextInput, Button, FlatList, StyleSheet } from 'react-native';


const reducer = (state, action) => {
  switch (action.type) {
    case 'ADD_TASK':
      return [...state, { id: Date.now(), text: action.payload }];
    case 'REMOVE_TASK':
      return state.filter((task) => task.id !== action.payload);
    default:
```

```
      return state;
    }
};


const ToDoList = () => {
    const [tasks, dispatch] = useReducer(reducer, []);
    const [task, setTask] = React.useState('');

    const addTask = () => {
        if (task.trim()) {
            dispatch({ type: 'ADD_TASK', payload: task });
            setTask('');
        }
    };


    return (
        <View style={styles.container}>
            <TextInput
                style={styles.input}
                value={task}
                onChangeText={setTask}
                placeholder="Enter a task"
```

```
                />
            <Button title="Add Task" onPress={addTask} />
            <FlatList
                data={tasks}
                keyExtractor={(item) => item.id.toString()}
                renderItem={({ item }) => (
                    <Text style={styles.task} onPress={() =>
dispatch({ type: 'REMOVE_TASK', payload: item.id })}>
                        {item.text}
                    </Text>
                )}
            />
        </View>
    );
};


const styles = StyleSheet.create({
    container: {
        flex: 1,
        padding: 20,
    },
    input: {
```

```
    borderWidth: 1,

    padding: 10,

    marginBottom: 10,

  },

  task: {

    padding: 10,

    backgroundColor: '#f0f0f0',

    marginVertical: 5,

  },

});


export default ToDoList;
```

Advantages:

- Handles complex state logic with ease.
- Encourages a clean separation of actions and updates.

---

3. Global State Management

When multiple components or screens need to share state, local state management becomes impractical. This is where **global state** comes into play.

3.1 Using the Context API

The Context API is built into React and allows you to share state across your component tree without prop drilling.

Example: Theme Context

javascript

```javascript
import React, { useContext, useState } from 'react';
import { View, Text, Button, StyleSheet } from 'react-native';

const ThemeContext = React.createContext();

const App = () => {
  const [theme, setTheme] = useState('light');

  return (
    <ThemeContext.Provider value={{ theme, setTheme }}>
      <HomeScreen />
    </ThemeContext.Provider>
  );
};

const HomeScreen = () => {
```

```
  const { theme, setTheme } =
useContext(ThemeContext);


  return (
    <View style={[styles.container, { backgroundColor:
theme === 'light' ? '#fff' : '#333' }]}>
      <Text style={{ color: theme === 'light' ? '#000' :
'#fff' }}>Current Theme: {theme}</Text>
      <Button
        title="Toggle Theme"
        onPress={() => setTheme(theme === 'light' ?
'dark' : 'light')}
      />
    </View>
  );
};


const styles = StyleSheet.create({
  container: {
    flex: 1,
    justifyContent: 'center',
    alignItems: 'center',
  },
```

```
});
```

export default App;

Advantages:

- Built into React (no additional libraries needed).

- Great for simple global state use cases.

Limitations:

- Not ideal for managing deeply nested or highly dynamic state.

---

4. Advanced State Management with Redux

Redux is a powerful state management library often used in large-scale applications. It centralizes state in a **store**, enabling predictable state updates through actions and reducers.

Core Concepts of Redux

1. **Store**: Holds the application's state.

2. **Actions**: Plain JavaScript objects describing changes.

3. **Reducers**: Pure functions that determine how the state changes in response to actions.

Installing Redux

bash

npm install redux react-redux

Example: Counter with Redux

1. **Create a Reducer**

javascript

```javascript
const initialState = { count: 0 };

const counterReducer = (state = initialState, action) => {
  switch (action.type) {
    case 'INCREMENT':
      return { count: state.count + 1 };
    case 'DECREMENT':
      return { count: state.count - 1 };
    default:
      return state;
  }
};
```

2. **Set Up the Store**

javascript

```javascript
import { createStore } from 'redux';
import { Provider } from 'react-redux';

const store = createStore(counterReducer);

const App = () => (
  <Provider store={store}>
    <Counter />
  </Provider>
);
```

3. **Connect Components**

javascript

```javascript
import { useSelector, useDispatch } from 'react-redux';

const Counter = () => {
  const count = useSelector((state) => state.count);
  const dispatch = useDispatch();

  return (
    <View>
      <Text>Count: {count}</Text>
```

```
      <Button title="Increase" onPress={() => dispatch({
type: 'INCREMENT' })} />

      <Button title="Decrease" onPress={() => dispatch({
type: 'DECREMENT' })} />

    </View>

  );

};
```

Advantages:

- Predictable state updates.
- Scalable for large applications.

Limitations:

- Boilerplate code can be overwhelming for small projects.

---

5. Alternatives to Redux

Redux is powerful but might be overkill for simpler applications. Here are two popular alternatives:

5.1 Zustand

Zustand is a lightweight state management library with minimal boilerplate.

Example: Counter with Zustand

javascript

```
import create from 'zustand';

const useStore = create((set) => ({
  count: 0,
  increment: () => set((state) => ({ count: state.count + 1
})),
  decrement: () => set((state) => ({ count: state.count - 1
})),
}));

const Counter = () => {
  const { count, increment, decrement } = useStore();

  return (
    <View>
      <Text>Count: {count}</Text>
      <Button title="Increase" onPress={increment} />
      <Button title="Decrease" onPress={decrement} />
    </View>
  );
};
```

Advantages:

- Minimal setup and boilerplate.

- Great for small to medium applications.

5.2 React Query

React Query is designed for managing server-state, making it an excellent choice for apps that heavily rely on APIs.

Example: Fetching Data with React Query

bash

```bash
npm install @tanstack/react-query
```

javascript

```javascript
import { useQuery } from '@tanstack/react-query';

const fetchTasks = async () => {
    const response = await fetch('https://jsonplaceholder.typicode.com/todos');
    return response.json();
};

const TaskList = () => {
```

```
const { data, isLoading } = useQuery(['tasks'],
fetchTasks);

if (isLoading) return <Text>Loading...</Text>;

return (
  <FlatList
    data={data}
    keyExtractor={(item) => item.id.toString()}
    renderItem={({ item }) =>
<Text>{item.title}</Text>}
    />
  );
};
```

Advantages:

- Optimized for API-based state.

- Simplifies caching and synchronization.

Chapter 8: Working with APIs and Data

Modern mobile applications often rely on external APIs to fetch data, whether it's displaying a list of products, fetching user information, or showing live weather updates. In this chapter, we'll learn how to work with APIs in React Native using **Axios** and the **Fetch API**, display fetched data with FlatList and SectionList, and handle common challenges like **error handling** and **loading states**.

---

1. Fetching Data with Axios and Fetch API

APIs enable your app to communicate with external servers and fetch dynamic data. React Native provides multiple ways to interact with APIs, with the most common being the **Fetch API** (built-in) and **Axios** (a third-party library).

1.1 Fetching Data with the Fetch API

The Fetch API is a browser-native method for making HTTP requests and is included in React Native by default.

Example: Fetching a List of Users

javascript

```javascript
import React, { useState, useEffect } from 'react';
import { View, Text, FlatList, StyleSheet } from 'react-native';

const App = () => {
  const [users, setUsers] = useState([]);
  const [loading, setLoading] = useState(true);

  useEffect(() => {
    const fetchData = async () => {
      try {
        const response = await fetch('https://jsonplaceholder.typicode.com/users');
        const data = await response.json();
        setUsers(data);
      } catch (error) {
        console.error('Error fetching users:', error);
      } finally {
```

```
      setLoading(false);
    }
  };


  fetchData();
}, []);


if (loading) return <Text>Loading...</Text>;


return (
  <FlatList
    data={users}
    keyExtractor={(item) => item.id.toString()}
    renderItem={({ item }) => (
      <Text style={styles.item}>{item.name}</Text>
    )}
  />
);
};


const styles = StyleSheet.create({
  item: {
```

```
        padding: 10,

        fontSize: 18,

        borderBottomWidth: 1,

        borderBottomColor: '#ccc',

    },

});
```

export default App;

Advantages of Fetch API:

- No additional libraries required.

- Simple syntax for basic requests.

Limitations:

- Requires manual handling of errors and timeouts.

- No built-in support for request cancellation.

1.2 Fetching Data with Axios

Axios is a powerful library for making HTTP requests, offering features like automatic JSON parsing, request cancellation, and interceptors.

Installation:

bash

npm install axios

Example: Fetching a List of Posts

javascript

```javascript
import React, { useState, useEffect } from 'react';
import { View, Text, FlatList, StyleSheet } from 'react-native';
import axios from 'axios';


const App = () => {
  const [posts, setPosts] = useState([]);
  const [loading, setLoading] = useState(true);

  useEffect(() => {
    const fetchPosts = async () => {
      try {
        const response = await axios.get('https://jsonplaceholder.typicode.com/posts');
        setPosts(response.data);
      } catch (error) {
        console.error('Error fetching posts:', error);
      } finally {
        setLoading(false);
```

```
      }
    };


    fetchPosts();
  }, []);


  if (loading) return <Text>Loading...</Text>;


  return (
    <FlatList
      data={posts}
      keyExtractor={(item) => item.id.toString()}
      renderItem={({ item }) => (
        <Text style={styles.item}>{item.title}</Text>
      )}
    />
  );
};


const styles = StyleSheet.create({
  item: {
    padding: 10,
```

```
    fontSize: 18,

    borderBottomWidth: 1,

    borderBottomColor: '#ccc',

  },

});
```

export default App;

Advantages of Axios:

- Automatically transforms JSON responses.
- Supports advanced features like interceptors and cancellation.
- Handles errors more gracefully than Fetch.

---

2. Displaying Data with FlatList and SectionList

Once you fetch data from an API, you'll often need to display it in a scrollable list. React Native provides two powerful components for this purpose: FlatList and SectionList.

2.1 Displaying Lists with FlatList

FlatList is optimized for rendering large datasets efficiently by only rendering the visible items.

Example: Displaying a List of Products

javascript

```javascript
import React, { useState, useEffect } from 'react';
import { View, Text, FlatList, StyleSheet } from 'react-native';
import axios from 'axios';

const App = () => {
  const [products, setProducts] = useState([]);

  useEffect(() => {
    const fetchProducts = async () => {
      const response = await axios.get('https://fakestoreapi.com/products');
      setProducts(response.data);
    };

    fetchProducts();
  }, []);

  return (
    <FlatList
```

```
      data={products}
      keyExtractor={(item) => item.id.toString()}
      renderItem={({ item }) => (
        <View style={styles.item}>
          <Text style={styles.title}>{item.title}</Text>
          <Text
style={styles.price}>${item.price}</Text>
        </View>
      )}
    />
  );
};


const styles = StyleSheet.create({
  item: {
    padding: 10,
    borderBottomWidth: 1,
    borderBottomColor: '#ccc',
  },
  title: {
    fontSize: 16,
    fontWeight: 'bold',
```

```
    },

  price: {

    fontSize: 14,

    color: 'green',

  },

});
```

export default App;

Advantages:

- Automatically handles scrolling.
- Supports performance optimizations like lazy loading (onEndReached).

2.2 Displaying Grouped Data with SectionList

SectionList is used for grouped or categorized data. It allows headers to be displayed for each section.

Example: Displaying Contacts Grouped by Letter

javascript

```
import React from 'react';

import { View, Text, SectionList, StyleSheet } from 'react-native';
```

```
const App = () => {
  const contacts = [
    { title: 'A', data: ['Alice', 'Albert'] },
    { title: 'B', data: ['Bob', 'Bella'] },
    { title: 'C', data: ['Charlie', 'Cindy'] },
  ];

  return (
    <SectionList
      sections={contacts}
      keyExtractor={(item, index) => item + index}
      renderItem={({ item }) => <Text
style={styles.item}>{item}</Text>}
      renderSectionHeader={({ section: { title } }) => (
        <Text style={styles.header}>{title}</Text>
      )}
    />
  );
};

const styles = StyleSheet.create({
```

```
  header: {

    fontSize: 18,

    fontWeight: 'bold',

    backgroundColor: '#eee',

    padding: 5,

  },

  item: {

    padding: 10,

    fontSize: 16,

  },

});
```

export default App;

Advantages:

- Ideal for categorized data.

- Supports headers for each section.

---

3. Error Handling and Loading States

Fetching data from APIs is prone to errors such as network issues, incorrect endpoints, or server downtime. Proper error handling ensures a smooth user experience.

3.1 Implementing Loading States

Always provide feedback when data is loading.

Example: Adding a Loading Indicator

javascript

```javascript
import React, { useState, useEffect } from 'react';
import { View, Text, ActivityIndicator, FlatList } from 'react-native';

const App = () => {
  const [data, setData] = useState([]);
  const [loading, setLoading] = useState(true);

  useEffect(() => {
    const fetchData = async () => {
      try {
        const response = await fetch('https://jsonplaceholder.typicode.com/posts');
        const result = await response.json();
        setData(result);
      } catch (error) {
        console.error('Error fetching data:', error);
      } finally {
```

```
      setLoading(false);

    }

  };


  fetchData();

}, []);


if (loading) return <ActivityIndicator size="large"
color="#0000ff" />;


return (
  <FlatList

    data={data}

    keyExtractor={(item) => item.id.toString()}

    renderItem={({ item }) =>
<Text>{item.title}</Text>}

    />

  );

};


export default App;
```

3.2 Handling API Errors

Provide meaningful error messages when an API request fails.

Example: Adding Error Handling

javascript

```
import React, { useState, useEffect } from 'react';
import { View, Text, Button, ActivityIndicator } from 'react-native';

const App = () => {
    const [data, setData] = useState(null);
    const [loading, setLoading] = useState(true);
    const [error, setError] = useState(null);

    const fetchData = async () => {
        setLoading(true);
        setError(null);

        try {
            const response = await fetch('https://jsonplaceholder.typicode.com/posts');

            if (!response.ok) throw new Error('Failed to fetch data');
```

```
      const result = await response.json();

      setData(result);

  } catch (err) {

      setError(err.message);

  } finally {

      setLoading(false);

  }

};


useEffect(() => {

  fetchData();

}, []);


if (loading) return <ActivityIndicator size="large"
color="#0000ff" />;


if (error) return (

  <View>

      <Text>Error: {error}</Text>

      <Button title="Retry" onPress={fetchData} />

  </View>

);
```

```
  return <Text>Data fetched successfully</Text>;
};


export default App;
```

Chapter 9: Handling User Input

Handling user input is essential for creating interactive mobile applications. From capturing text in forms to validating user entries and implementing gestures for touch interactions, React Native offers a range of tools and libraries to simplify the process. This chapter will cover how to use TextInput for forms, validate input using custom logic or libraries like **Yup**, and handle gestures with **React Native Gesture Handler**.

---

1. TextInput and Forms

Forms are a core part of mobile apps, enabling users to submit information like login credentials, feedback, or search queries. React Native's TextInput component is a versatile tool for creating form fields.

1.1 Using TextInput

TextInput is a core React Native component for capturing text input.

Example: Basic TextInput

javascript

```jsx
import React, { useState } from 'react';
import { View, TextInput, Text, StyleSheet } from 'react-native';


const App = () => {
  const [value, setValue] = useState('');


  return (
    <View style={styles.container}>
      <Text style={styles.label}>Enter your name:</Text>
      <TextInput
        style={styles.input}
        placeholder="Type here..."
        value={value}
        onChangeText={(text) => setValue(text)}
      />
      <Text style={styles.output}>Hello, {value}!</Text>
    </View>
  );
};
```

```
const styles = StyleSheet.create({
  container: {
    padding: 20,
  },
  label: {
    fontSize: 18,
    marginBottom: 10,
  },
  input: {
    height: 40,
    borderColor: 'gray',
    borderWidth: 1,
    padding: 10,
    marginBottom: 10,
  },
  output: {
    fontSize: 18,
    marginTop: 10,
  },
});

export default App;
```

1.2 Handling Multiple Inputs

You can manage multiple TextInput components by using a single state object.

Example: Login Form

javascript

```javascript
import React, { useState } from 'react';
import { View, TextInput, Button, StyleSheet, Text } from 'react-native';

const App = () => {
  const [formData, setFormData] = useState({ username: '', password: '' });

  const handleChange = (name, value) => {
    setFormData((prev) => ({ ...prev, [name]: value }));
  };

  const handleSubmit = () => {
    console.log('Form Data:', formData);
  };
```

```jsx
  return (
    <View style={styles.container}>
      <Text style={styles.label}>Username:</Text>
      <TextInput
        style={styles.input}
        placeholder="Enter username"
        value={formData.username}
        onChangeText={(text) =>
handleChange('username', text)}
      />
      <Text style={styles.label}>Password:</Text>
      <TextInput
        style={styles.input}
        placeholder="Enter password"
        secureTextEntry
        value={formData.password}
        onChangeText={(text) =>
handleChange('password', text)}
      />
      <Button title="Submit" onPress={handleSubmit} />
    </View>
  );
};
```

```
const styles = StyleSheet.create({
    container: {
        padding: 20,
    },
    label: {
        fontSize: 18,
        marginBottom: 10,
    },
    input: {
        height: 40,
        borderColor: 'gray',
        borderWidth: 1,
        padding: 10,
        marginBottom: 20,
    },
});


export default App;
```

---

2. Validating Input

Form validation ensures users provide correct and meaningful data. You can validate inputs using custom logic or libraries like **Yup**.

2.1 Custom Validation Logic

Custom validation logic can be implemented within your component.

Example: Basic Email Validation

javascript

```javascript
import React, { useState } from 'react';
import { View, TextInput, Text, Button, StyleSheet } from 'react-native';

const App = () => {
  const [email, setEmail] = useState('');
  const [error, setError] = useState('');

  const validateEmail = () => {
    const emailRegex = /^[^\s@]+@[^\s@]+\.[^\s@]+$/;
    if (!emailRegex.test(email)) {
      setError('Invalid email format');
```

```
    } else {
      setError('');
      console.log('Valid email:', email);
    }
  };


  return (
    <View style={styles.container}>
      <TextInput
        style={styles.input}
        placeholder="Enter your email"
        value={email}
        onChangeText={setEmail}
      />
      {error ? <Text style={styles.error}>{error}</Text>
: null}
      <Button title="Validate" onPress={validateEmail}
/>
    </View>
  );
};


const styles = StyleSheet.create({
```

```
container: {
  padding: 20,
},
input: {
  height: 40,
  borderColor: 'gray',
  borderWidth: 1,
  padding: 10,
  marginBottom: 10,
},
error: {
  color: 'red',
  marginBottom: 10,
},
});

export default App;
```

2.2 Validating Input with Yup

Yup is a schema-based validation library that works seamlessly with form management libraries like Formik.

Installation:

```bash
npm install yup
```

Example: Using Yup for Validation

```javascript
import React, { useState } from 'react';
import { View, TextInput, Button, StyleSheet, Text } from 'react-native';
import * as Yup from 'yup';

const validationSchema = Yup.object().shape({
  username: Yup.string().required('Username is required'),
  password: Yup.string()
    .required('Password is required')
    .min(6, 'Password must be at least 6 characters'),
});

const App = () => {
  const [formData, setFormData] = useState({ username: '', password: '' });
  const [errors, setErrors] = useState({});
```

```javascript
const validate = async () => {
    try {
        await validationSchema.validate(formData, {
abortEarly: false });
        setErrors({});
        console.log('Form is valid:', formData);
    } catch (err) {
        const formattedErrors = {};
        err.inner.forEach((error) => {
            formattedErrors[error.path] = error.message;
        });
        setErrors(formattedErrors);
    }
};


return (
    <View style={styles.container}>
        <TextInput
            style={styles.input}
            placeholder="Username"
            value={formData.username}
            onChangeText={(text) => setFormData({
...formData, username: text })}
```

```jsx
        />
        {errors.username && <Text
style={styles.error}>{errors.username}</Text>}
        <TextInput
          style={styles.input}
          placeholder="Password"
          secureTextEntry
          value={formData.password}
          onChangeText={(text) => setFormData({
...formData, password: text })}
        />
        {errors.password && <Text
style={styles.error}>{errors.password}</Text>}
        <Button title="Submit" onPress={validate} />
      </View>
  );
};


const styles = StyleSheet.create({
  container: {
    padding: 20,
  },
  input: {
```

```
    height: 40,

    borderColor: 'gray',

    borderWidth: 1,

    padding: 10,

    marginBottom: 10,

  },

  error: {

    color: 'red',

    marginBottom: 10,

  },

});


export default App;
```

3. Gesture Handling with React Native Gesture Handler

Gesture-based interactions (swipes, taps, long presses, etc.) are essential for creating a natural user experience in mobile apps. **React Native Gesture Handler** is a library optimized for handling gestures.

3.1 Installing Gesture Handler

Install and link the library:

bash

npm install react-native-gesture-handler

3.2 Handling Basic Gestures

Use built-in gesture components like TapGestureHandler to detect gestures.

Example: Tap Gesture

javascript

```javascript
import React from 'react';
import { View, Text, StyleSheet } from 'react-native';
import { TapGestureHandler } from 'react-native-gesture-handler';

const App = () => {
  const handleTap = () => {
    console.log('Screen tapped!');
  };

  return (
```

```
    <TapGestureHandler onActivated={handleTap}>
      <View style={styles.container}>
        <Text style={styles.text}>Tap anywhere on the
screen</Text>
      </View>
    </TapGestureHandler>
  );
};


const styles = StyleSheet.create({
  container: {
    flex: 1,
    justifyContent: 'center',
    alignItems: 'center',
    backgroundColor: '#f0f0f0',
  },
  text: {
    fontSize: 18,
  },
});

export default App;
```

3.3 Advanced Gestures

You can chain gestures like swipes and pinches using GestureDetector and Gesture APIs.

Example: Swipe Gesture

javascript

```javascript
import React from 'react';
import { View, Text, StyleSheet } from 'react-native';
import { GestureDetector, Gesture } from 'react-native-gesture-handler';

const App = () => {
  const swipeGesture = Gesture.Swipe()
    .direction(Gesture.Direction.LEFT)
    .onEnd(() => console.log('Swiped left!'));

  return (
    <GestureDetector gesture={swipeGesture}>
      <View style={styles.container}>
        <Text>Swipe Left</Text>
      </View>
    </GestureDetector>
```

```
    );
};


const styles = StyleSheet.create({
    container: {
        flex: 1,
        justifyContent: 'center',
        alignItems: 'center',
        backgroundColor: '#f9f9f9',
    },
});


export default App;
```

Chapter 10: Animations and User Experience

Animations are essential for creating engaging and intuitive user experiences in mobile apps. React Native provides powerful tools to animate components, manage transitions, and integrate advanced animations using third-party libraries. In this chapter, we'll explore:

1. Animating components with the **Animated API**.

2. Adding transition animations with **React Navigation**.

3. Using third-party libraries like **Reanimated** and **Lottie**.

---

1. Animating Components with the Animated API

React Native's Animated API is a versatile and powerful tool for animating component properties like position, scale, rotation, and opacity.

1.1 Basics of the Animated API

The Animated API supports two main types of animations:

- **Declarative Animations**: Use Animated.timing or other functions to define how a property changes over time.

- **Interpolations**: Map animated values to ranges for complex effects (e.g., scaling or color transitions).

Example: Fade-In Animation

javascript

```javascript
import React, { useRef, useEffect } from 'react';
import { View, Text, Animated, StyleSheet } from 'react-native';


const App = () => {
  const fadeAnim = useRef(new Animated.Value(0)).current; // Initial opacity: 0


  useEffect(() => {
    Animated.timing(fadeAnim, {
      toValue: 1, // Final opacity
      duration: 2000,
      useNativeDriver: true, // Optimizes performance
```

```
    }).start();
  }, [fadeAnim]);


  return (
    <Animated.View style={[styles.box, { opacity:
fadeAnim }]}>
      <Text style={styles.text}>Hello,
Animation!</Text>
    </Animated.View>
  );
};


const styles = StyleSheet.create({
  box: {
    flex: 1,
    justifyContent: 'center',
    alignItems: 'center',
    backgroundColor: '#f0f0f0',
  },
  text: {
    fontSize: 24,
  },
});
```

```javascript
export default App;
```

1.2 Animating Position

Move components across the screen by animating their position using Animated.Value for translateX or translateY.

Example: Sliding Animation

javascript

```javascript
const slideAnim = useRef(new Animated.Value(-100)).current; // Start position off-screen

useEffect(() => {
    Animated.timing(slideAnim, {
        toValue: 0, // Move to on-screen position
        duration: 1000,
        useNativeDriver: true,
    }).start();
}, [slideAnim]);

return (
    <Animated.View style={{ transform: [{ translateX: slideAnim }] }}>
```

```
  <Text style={styles.text}>Slide In</Text>
  </Animated.View>
);
```

1.3 Combining Animations

Use Animated.parallel or Animated.sequence to run multiple animations simultaneously or in sequence.

Example: Combined Animations

javascript

```
useEffect(() => {
  Animated.sequence([
    Animated.timing(fadeAnim, {
      toValue: 1,
      duration: 1000,
      useNativeDriver: true,
    }),
    Animated.timing(slideAnim, {
      toValue: 0,
      duration: 1000,
      useNativeDriver: true,
    }),
```

```javascript
]).start();

}, [fadeAnim, slideAnim]);
```

---

2. Transition Animations with React Navigation

React Navigation automatically handles screen transitions like sliding between screens or fading. However, you can customize these transitions for a more dynamic experience.

2.1 Default Transitions

When using React Navigation, stack navigators provide built-in transitions like sliding from the right (iOS) or fading (Android).

Example: Basic Navigation

javascript

```javascript
import { createStackNavigator } from '@react-navigation/stack';

import { NavigationContainer } from '@react-navigation/native';


const Stack = createStackNavigator();
```

```javascript
export default function App() {

  return (

    <NavigationContainer>

      <Stack.Navigator>

        <Stack.Screen name="Home"
component={HomeScreen} />

        <Stack.Screen name="Details"
component={DetailsScreen} />

      </Stack.Navigator>

    </NavigationContainer>

  );

}
```

2.2 Customizing Transitions

Override default transitions by passing screenOptions or using a custom transition spec.

Example: Custom Slide Transition

javascript

```javascript
import { CardStyleInterpolators } from '@react-
navigation/stack';


<Stack.Navigator
```

```jsx
  screenOptions={{

    cardStyleInterpolator:
CardStyleInterpolators.forHorizontalIOS,

  }}
>

  <Stack.Screen name="Home"
component={HomeScreen} />

  <Stack.Screen name="Details"
component={DetailsScreen} />

</Stack.Navigator>;
```

2.3 Shared Element Transitions

For advanced animations like transitioning an image or element between screens, you can use libraries like **React Navigation Shared Element**.

Example: Shared Image Transition

javascript

```javascript
import { createSharedElementStackNavigator } from 'react-navigation-shared-element';


const SharedStack =
createSharedElementStackNavigator();
```

```
<SharedStack.Navigator>

  <SharedStack.Screen name="List"
component={ListScreen} />

  <SharedStack.Screen

    name="Detail"

    component={DetailScreen}

    sharedElements={(route) => {

      const { item } = route.params;

      return [`item.${item.id}`];

    }}

  />

</SharedStack.Navigator>;
```

---

3. Third-Party Animation Libraries

Third-party libraries like **Reanimated** and **Lottie** offer enhanced performance and features for complex animations.

3.1 Using React Native Reanimated

Reanimated provides an improved performance model for animations by offloading calculations to the native thread.

Installation:

bash

npm install react-native-reanimated

Example: Animated Button with Reanimated

javascript

```
import React from 'react';
import { View, Text, StyleSheet } from 'react-native';
import Animated, { useSharedValue, useAnimatedStyle,
withSpring } from 'react-native-reanimated';

const App = () => {
  const scale = useSharedValue(1);

  const animatedStyle = useAnimatedStyle(() => ({
    transform: [{ scale: scale.value }],
  }));

  return (
    <View style={styles.container}>
```

```jsx
      <Animated.View style={[styles.button,
animatedStyle]}>

        <Text

          style={styles.text}

          onPress={() => (scale.value =
withSpring(scale.value === 1 ? 1.5 : 1))}

        >

          Press Me

        </Text>

      </Animated.View>

    </View>

  );

};


const styles = StyleSheet.create({

  container: {

    flex: 1,

    justifyContent: 'center',

    alignItems: 'center',

  },

  button: {

    backgroundColor: 'blue',

    padding: 20,
```

```
      borderRadius: 10,
    },
    text: {
      color: 'white',
      fontSize: 16,
    },
  });


export default App;
```

Advantages of Reanimated:

- Runs animations on the native thread for smoother performance.

- Supports gestures via integration with Gesture Handler.

3.2 Using Lottie for Animated Graphics

Lottie is a library for rendering beautiful animations exported from Adobe After Effects as JSON files.

Installation:

bash

```
npm install lottie-react-native
```

Example: Adding a Loading Animation

javascript

```javascript
import React from 'react';
import { View, StyleSheet } from 'react-native';
import LottieView from 'lottie-react-native';


const App = () => {
  return (
    <View style={styles.container}>
      <LottieView
        source={require('./loading.json')} // Replace with your animation file
        autoPlay
        loop
      />
    </View>
  );
};


const styles = StyleSheet.create({
```

```
    container: {

      flex: 1,

      justifyContent: 'center',

      alignItems: 'center',

    },

  });


export default App;
```

Advantages of Lottie:

- Easily integrates high-quality animations.
- Simplifies the process of adding intricate designs.

Chapter 11: Integrating Native Modules

React Native enables developers to build mobile apps using JavaScript, but there are scenarios where you need to interact with platform-specific features or use native code for optimal performance. This chapter will explore **bridging native code in React Native** for both Android and iOS using Java, Swift, and Objective-C. We'll also demonstrate how to integrate device-specific functionality such as the camera and GPS.

---

1. Understanding Native Modules

A **native module** is a bridge that connects JavaScript to native platform APIs. React Native uses this bridge to communicate between JavaScript and native code (Java for Android, Swift/Objective-C for iOS).

- **When to Use Native Modules**:

    o Access device-specific APIs unavailable in React Native.

    o Optimize performance for computationally heavy tasks.

    o Extend app functionality using third-party native libraries.

2. Bridging Native Code in React Native

2.1 Bridging in Android (Java)

Native modules in Android are written in Java or Kotlin. Let's create a simple module to demonstrate bridging.

Example: Creating a Toast Module in Android

1. **Create the Native Module**:

   - Open the Android directory of your React Native project in Android Studio.

   - Navigate to android/app/src/main/java/com/<your_app_name> and create a new file ToastModule.java.

java

```java
package com.your_app_name;


import android.widget.Toast;

import com.facebook.react.bridge.ReactApplicationContext;

import com.facebook.react.bridge.ReactContextBaseJavaModule;
```

```java
import com.facebook.react.bridge.ReactMethod;

public class ToastModule extends
ReactContextBaseJavaModule {
    private static ReactApplicationContext reactContext;

    public ToastModule(ReactApplicationContext context) {
        super(context);
        reactContext = context;
    }

    @Override
    public String getName() {
        return "ToastModule";
    }

    @ReactMethod
    public void showToast(String message, int duration) {
        Toast.makeText(reactContext, message,
duration).show();
    }
}
```

2. **Register the Module**:

- o Add the module to the package manager by creating a CustomPackage.java file.

java

```java
package com.your_app_name;

import com.facebook.react.ReactPackage;
import com.facebook.react.bridge.NativeModule;
import com.facebook.react.uimanager.ViewManager;

import java.util.ArrayList;
import java.util.Collections;
import java.util.List;

public class CustomPackage implements ReactPackage {
    @Override
    public List<NativeModule> createNativeModules(ReactApplicationContext reactContext) {
        List<NativeModule> modules = new ArrayList<>();
        modules.add(new ToastModule(reactContext));
        return modules;
    }
}
```

```java
    @Override

    public List<ViewManager>
createViewManagers(ReactApplicationContext
reactContext) {

        return Collections.emptyList();

    }

}
```

3. **Update MainApplication.java:**

   o Register the custom package in
     android/app/src/main/java/com/<your_app_
     name>/MainApplication.java.

java

```java
@Override

protected List<ReactPackage> getPackages() {

    return Arrays.<ReactPackage>asList(

      new MainReactPackage(),

      new CustomPackage() // Add this line

    );

}
```

4. **Use the Module in JavaScript:**

   o Access the module using NativeModules.

javascript

```javascript
import { NativeModules } from 'react-native';
const { ToastModule } = NativeModules;


ToastModule.showToast('Hello from Native Code!', ToastModule.SHORT);
```

2.2 Bridging in iOS (Swift/Objective-C)

On iOS, native modules are written in Swift or Objective-C. Let's create a simple module to demonstrate bridging.

Example: Creating a Toast Module in iOS

1. **Create the Native Module**:
   - In Xcode, navigate to the ios directory of your project and create a new Swift file named ToastModule.swift.

swift

```swift
import Foundation
import UIKit


@objc(ToastModule)
class ToastModule: NSObject {
```

```swift
@objc
func showToast(_ message: String, duration: Double) {
    DispatchQueue.main.async {
        let toast = UILabel()
        toast.text = message
        toast.alpha = 1.0
        toast.backgroundColor =
UIColor.black.withAlphaComponent(0.6)
        toast.textColor = UIColor.white
        toast.textAlignment = .center
        toast.layer.cornerRadius = 10
        toast.clipsToBounds = true
        let appDelegate = UIApplication.shared.delegate
        let window = appDelegate?.window!
        toast.frame = CGRect(x: 20, y:
window!.frame.height - 100, width: window!.frame.width -
40, height: 50)
        window?.addSubview(toast)
        UIView.animate(withDuration: duration,
animations: {
            toast.alpha = 0.0
        }) { (_) in
            toast.removeFromSuperview()
```

```
        }
      }
    }
}
```

2. **Register the Module**:
   - Add a bridging header file if it doesn't exist (YourApp-Bridging-Header.h) and register the module in AppDelegate.m.

objective

```
#import "React/RCTBridgeModule.h"
```

3. **Expose the Module to React Native**:
   - Add the following line in ToastModule.swift:

swift

```
@objc(ToastModule)
class ToastModule: NSObject {
  static func requiresMainQueueSetup() -> Bool {
    return true
  }
}
```

4. **Use the Module in JavaScript**:

javascript

```javascript
import { NativeModules } from 'react-native';
const { ToastModule } = NativeModules;


ToastModule.showToast('Hello from Swift!', 2.0);
```

---

3. Examples of Integrating Device-Specific Functionality

React Native provides libraries for common device-specific features, but custom native code may be necessary for advanced use cases. Let's explore two popular scenarios: accessing the **camera** and **GPS**.

3.1 Camera Integration

You can use the react-native-camera library for accessing the device's camera.

Installation:

bash

```bash
npm install react-native-camera
```

Example: Using the Camera

javascript

```javascript
import React from 'react';
import { View, StyleSheet } from 'react-native';
import { RNCamera } from 'react-native-camera';

const CameraApp = () => {
  let camera;

  const takePicture = async () => {
    if (camera) {
      const options = { quality: 0.5, base64: true };
      const data = await
camera.takePictureAsync(options);
      console.log(data.uri);
    }
  };

  return (
    <RNCamera
      ref={(ref) => (camera = ref)}
```

```
        style={styles.preview}

        type={RNCamera.Constants.Type.back}

        captureAudio={false}

      >

        <View style={styles.capture}
onTouchEnd={takePicture} />

      </RNCamera>

    );

};


const styles = StyleSheet.create({

    preview: {

        flex: 1,

        justifyContent: 'flex-end',

        alignItems: 'center',

    },

    capture: {

        flex: 0,

        backgroundColor: '#fff',

        borderRadius: 5,

        padding: 15,

        margin: 20,
```

```
    },
});
```

export default CameraApp;

3.2 GPS Integration

For GPS, you can use the react-native-geolocation-service library.

Installation:

bash

```
npm install react-native-geolocation-service
```

Example: Accessing Location

javascript

```javascript
import React, { useState, useEffect } from 'react';
import { View, Text, Button, PermissionsAndroid,
Platform } from 'react-native';
import Geolocation from 'react-native-geolocation-service';

const GPSApp = () => {
```

```javascript
const [location, setLocation] = useState(null);

const requestLocationPermission = async () => {
    if (Platform.OS === 'android') {
        const granted = await PermissionsAndroid.request(

PermissionsAndroid.PERMISSIONS.ACCESS_FINE_LO
CATION
        );
        return granted ===
PermissionsAndroid.RESULTS.GRANTED;
    }
    return true;
};

const getLocation = async () => {
    const hasPermission = await
requestLocationPermission();
    if (hasPermission) {
        Geolocation.getCurrentPosition(
            (position) => {
                setLocation(position.coords);
            },
```

```
      (error) => {
        console.error(error);
      },
      { enableHighAccuracy: true, timeout: 15000 }
    );
  }
};


useEffect(() => {
  getLocation();
}, []);


return (
  <View>
    <Text>Latitude: {location?.latitude}</Text>
    <Text>Longitude: {location?.longitude}</Text>
    <Button title="Refresh Location"
onPress={getLocation} />
  </View>
);
};
```

export default GPSApp;

---

4. Testing and Debugging Native Modules

When working with native modules:

- **Debugging on Android**: Use Android Studio's logcat to debug errors in Java.

- **Debugging on iOS**: Use Xcode's debug console and inspect native logs.

- **Unit Testing**: Write test cases for native modules using Jest or Detox.

Chapter 12: Testing Your App

Testing is a crucial part of mobile app development to ensure your application works as intended and provides a seamless user experience. In this chapter, we'll explore:

1. **Unit Testing** with Jest.

2. **UI Testing** with Detox or Appium.

3. **Continuous Integration (CI) Strategies** to automate testing workflows.

---

1. Unit Testing with Jest

1.1 What is Unit Testing?

Unit testing focuses on testing individual pieces of logic in isolation, such as functions, components, or hooks. This ensures that each piece works as expected.

1.2 Setting Up Jest

Jest is a JavaScript testing framework that comes with built-in support for React Native.

Installation:

bash

```
npm install --save-dev jest react-test-renderer @testing-
library/react-native
```

Configure Jest in your package.json:

json

```json
"jest": {
    "preset": "react-native"
}
```

1.3 Writing Unit Tests

Example: Testing a Utility Function

Create a utility function add.js:

javascript

```javascript
export const add = (a, b) => a + b;
```

Write a test in add.test.js:

javascript

```javascript
import { add } from './add';

test('adds two numbers', () => {
    expect(add(2, 3)).toBe(5);
```

```
});
```

Run the test:

bash

```
npm test
```

Example: Testing a React Component

Component Greeting.js:

javascript

```
import React from 'react';
import { Text } from 'react-native';

const Greeting = ({ name }) => <Text>Hello, {name}!</Text>;

export default Greeting;
```

Test for Greeting:

javascript

```
import React from 'react';
import { render } from '@testing-library/react-native';
import Greeting from './Greeting';
```

```
test('renders greeting correctly', () => {

    const { getByText } = render(<Greeting name="John" />);

    expect(getByText('Hello, John!')).toBeTruthy();

});
```

---

2. UI Testing with Detox or Appium

2.1 What is UI Testing?

UI testing ensures that your app's user interface behaves correctly, simulating user interactions like button presses, swipes, and screen transitions.

2.2 Detox for UI Testing

What is Detox? Detox is an end-to-end testing framework designed for React Native, focusing on automating UI tests and validating app behavior in real devices or simulators.

Installation:

bash

npm install --save-dev detox

detox init -r jest

Configure Detox: Edit the detox.config.js file:

```javascript
module.exports = {
  testRunner: 'jest',
  runnerConfig: 'e2e/config.json',
  configurations: {
    ios: {
      type: 'ios.simulator',
      binaryPath: 'ios/build/Build/Products/Debug-iphonesimulator/MyApp.app',
      build: 'xcodebuild -workspace ios/MyApp.xcworkspace -scheme MyApp -configuration Debug -sdk iphonesimulator',
    },
    android: {
      type: 'android.emulator',
      binaryPath: 'android/app/build/outputs/apk/debug/app-debug.apk',
      build: 'cd android && ./gradlew assembleDebug assembleAndroidTest && ./gradlew connectedAndroidTest',
    },
  },
};
```

Writing Detox Tests:

Create a test file e2e/firstTest.e2e.js:

javascript

```javascript
describe('App Launch', () => {
  beforeAll(async () => {
    await device.launchApp();
  });

  it('should show welcome screen', async () => {
    await expect(element(by.id('welcome'))).toBeVisible();
  });

  it('should navigate to next screen', async () => {
    await element(by.id('nextButton')).tap();
    await expect(element(by.id('nextScreen'))).toBeVisible();
  });
});
```

Run the test:

bash

detox test

2.3 Appium for UI Testing

What is Appium? Appium is a cross-platform UI automation framework that allows testing of mobile, web, and hybrid apps.

Installation: Install Appium globally:

bash

```
npm install -g appium
```

Writing Appium Tests:

Install WebDriver:

bash

```
npm install webdriverio
```

Create a test script appium.test.js:

javascript

```
const wdio = require('webdriverio');

const opts = {
    path: '/wd/hub',
    port: 4723,
```

```javascript
  capabilities: {
    platformName: 'Android',
    platformVersion: '10.0',
    deviceName: 'emulator-5554',
    app: '/path/to/app.apk',
    automationName: 'UiAutomator2',
  },
};

const main = async () => {
  const client = await wdio.remote(opts);

  const button = await client.$('~nextButton');
  await button.click();

  const nextScreen = await client.$('~nextScreen');
  console.log(await nextScreen.isDisplayed());

  await client.deleteSession();
};

main();
```

Run the script:

bash

node appium.test.js

---

3. Continuous Integration Strategies

Continuous Integration (CI) automates testing and deployment pipelines, ensuring that every code change is validated against your tests before merging.

3.1 Why Use CI?

- Automates testing workflows, reducing manual effort.
- Prevents broken code from reaching production.
- Provides consistent feedback to developers.

3.2 Setting Up CI with GitHub Actions

GitHub Actions is a popular CI/CD tool for automating workflows.

Create a CI Workflow File:

Add .github/workflows/ci.yml:

yaml

```yaml
name: React Native CI

on:
  push:
    branches:
      - main
  pull_request:
    branches:
      - main

jobs:
  test:
    runs-on: ubuntu-latest

    steps:
      - name: Checkout code
        uses: actions/checkout@v3

      - name: Set up Node.js
        uses: actions/setup-node@v3
        with:
```

```
        node-version: 16

    - name: Install dependencies

      run: npm install

    - name: Run unit tests

      run: npm test

    - name: Run UI tests

      run: detox test --configuration android
```

3.3 Setting Up CI with CircleCI

CircleCI is another widely used CI/CD tool, especially for mobile apps.

Create a CircleCI Config File:

Add .circleci/config.yml:

yaml

```
version: 2.1

jobs:
  build:
```

```yaml
    docker:
      - image: circleci/node:16

    steps:
      - checkout
      - run:
          name: Install dependencies
          command: npm install
      - run:
          name: Run unit tests
          command: npm test


  ui-test:
    docker:
      - image: circleci/android:api-30

    steps:
      - checkout
      - run:
          name: Build Detox APK
          command: cd android && ./gradlew assembleDebug assembleAndroidTest
```

```
- run:

  name: Run Detox tests

  command: detox test --configuration
android.emulator


workflows:

 version: 2

 test_and_build:

  jobs:

   - build

   - ui-test
```

3.4 Benefits of CI for React Native

- **Early Error Detection**: CI runs your tests on every pull request, catching issues before they reach production.

- **Automated Releases**: CI/CD pipelines can be extended to automate app deployment to app stores.

- **Scalability**: CI supports parallel testing across multiple devices and configurations.

Chapter 13: Performance Optimization

Performance optimization is essential to ensure React Native apps deliver a smooth, responsive, and efficient user experience. In this chapter, we'll explore how to profile performance using tools like **Flipper** and **React DevTools**, and implement strategies to optimize **image loading**, **memory usage**, and **UI responsiveness**.

---

1. Profiling Performance

Profiling helps identify performance bottlenecks by analyzing your app's behavior and resource usage.

1.1 Profiling with Flipper

What is Flipper? Flipper is a debugging tool for React Native apps that provides insights into logs, performance, and network usage.

Setting Up Flipper:

1. Install Flipper from the official website.

2. Ensure your React Native project supports Flipper:

o For React Native >= 0.62, Flipper is pre-
   integrated. Update dependencies with:

bash

```
npm install react-native-flipper
```

3. Launch Flipper and connect your device or
   emulator.

Using Flipper for Profiling:

- **Performance Monitoring**: Use the **Performance**
  plugin to measure app frame rates and detect
  dropped frames.

- **Network Analysis**: Inspect API calls using the
  Network plugin to track response times and
  payload sizes.

- **Logs**: Monitor application logs to debug issues in
  real-time.

1.2 Profiling with React DevTools

What are React DevTools? React DevTools allows you to
inspect the component tree, check prop/state values, and
monitor re-renders.

Installation:

bash

```
npm install --save-dev react-devtools
```

Run the DevTools:

bash

```
npx react-devtools
```

Profiling Steps:

1. Open React DevTools while running your app.

2. Switch to the **Profiler** tab.

3. Record interactions and analyze:

   o **Commit Time**: Time spent rendering updates.

   o **Re-render Frequency**: Identify components that re-render excessively.

Optimizing Re-renders:

- Use React.memo to prevent unnecessary re-renders for functional components.

- Use shouldComponentUpdate for class components.

- Profile with tools like **why-did-you-render** to identify unnecessary updates.

---

2. Optimizing Image Loading

Images are a common source of performance issues, as they consume memory and bandwidth. Optimizing image handling can drastically improve load times and memory usage.

2.1 Using Optimized Image Formats

Use Modern Formats:

- Prefer **WebP** or **HEIF** formats over traditional formats like JPEG and PNG, as they offer better compression.

Example: WebP Images

javascript

```
<Image source={{ uri: 'https://example.com/image.webp' }} style={{ width: 100, height: 100 }} />
```

Tools for Conversion:

- Use tools like Squoosh to compress images.

2.2 Lazy Loading and Caching

Lazy Loading:

- Load images only when they're about to appear on the screen using libraries like react-native-fast-image.

Caching Images:

- Use the react-native-fast-image library for advanced image caching.

Installation:

bash

npm install react-native-fast-image

Example: Using FastImage

javascript

```
import FastImage from 'react-native-fast-image';

<FastImage
    style={{ width: 200, height: 200 }}
    source={{
        uri: 'https://example.com/image.jpg',
        priority: FastImage.priority.high,
    }}
    resizeMode={FastImage.resizeMode.cover}
/>;
```

2.3 Resizing and Thumbnails

Resize images on the server side or generate thumbnails to minimize memory usage.

Example: Generating Thumbnails Instead of loading full-resolution images:

- Use a smaller version for initial rendering.

- Replace with the full-size image when needed.

javascript

```
<Image source={{ uri: 'https://example.com/thumbnail.jpg' }} style={{ width: 100, height: 100 }} />
```

---

3. Optimizing Memory Usage

Memory leaks and excessive memory consumption can lead to app crashes and poor performance. Here's how to manage memory effectively in React Native.

3.1 Avoid Memory Leaks

Memory leaks often occur when:

- Listeners or intervals are not cleaned up.

- Large datasets are stored in memory unnecessarily.

Best Practices:

- Remove event listeners in useEffect cleanup:

javascript

```javascript
useEffect(() => {

  const listener = someEvent.addListener(() => {});


  return () => {

    listener.remove();

  };

}, []);
```

- Use setState cautiously to avoid keeping references to unused data.

3.2 Efficient Data Handling

For large datasets, use optimized components like FlatList and SectionList instead of ScrollView.

Example: Optimized List Rendering

javascript

```javascript
import { FlatList } from 'react-native';


const App = () => {

  const data = Array.from({ length: 1000 }, (_, i) => `Item ${i}`);


  return (
```

```
<FlatList

  data={data}

  keyExtractor={(item, index) => index.toString()}

  renderItem={({ item }) => <Text>{item}</Text>}

/>

);

};
```

Advantages of FlatList:

- Lazy loads items.

- Reduces memory consumption by unmounting off-screen items.

---

4. Optimizing UI Responsiveness

Smooth UI interactions are critical for a good user experience. Delays, frame drops, or jittery animations degrade app quality.

4.1 Minimize JavaScript Thread Work

The JavaScript thread should handle minimal computation, as heavy tasks block UI updates.

Best Practices:

- Offload heavy computations to a background thread using libraries like react-native-workers.

- Optimize loops and avoid nested iterations in JavaScript.

4.2 Debouncing and Throttling

Debounce delays execution until the user has stopped triggering the event, reducing redundant calculations.

Throttle limits the frequency of function execution, ensuring smooth interactions.

Example: Debounce Search Input

javascript

```
import React, { useState } from 'react';

import { TextInput } from 'react-native';

import debounce from 'lodash.debounce';


const App = () => {

    const [query, setQuery] = useState('');


    const handleSearch = debounce((text) => {

        console.log('Searching for:', text);

    }, 500);


    return (
```

```
<TextInput

  placeholder="Search"

  onChangeText={(text) => {

    setQuery(text);

    handleSearch(text);

  }}

/>

);

};


export default App;
```

4.3 Optimizing Animations

Animations should run on the native thread to avoid
blocking UI updates.

Use Native Drivers:

- Use useNativeDriver: true for Animated API
  animations.

Example: Native Driver Animation

javascript


```
import React, { useRef, useEffect } from 'react';

import { Animated } from 'react-native';
```

```
const App = () => {

  const fadeAnim = useRef(new
Animated.Value(0)).current;


  useEffect(() => {

    Animated.timing(fadeAnim, {

      toValue: 1,

      duration: 1000,

      useNativeDriver: true,

    }).start();

  }, [fadeAnim]);


  return <Animated.View style={{ opacity: fadeAnim }}
/>;

};


export default App;
```

Third-Party Libraries:

- Use libraries like **React Native Reanimated** for smooth animations that leverage the native thread.

5. Tools for Monitoring and Debugging Performance

5.1 Use the Hermes Engine

Hermes is a lightweight JavaScript engine optimized for React Native, reducing startup time and improving memory usage.

Enabling Hermes:

1. Open android/app/build.gradle.
2. Set enableHermes: true:

gradle

```
project.ext.react = [

    enableHermes: true

]
```

5.2 Debugging with Flipper Plugins

Flipper offers plugins to debug:

- **Memory**: Inspect memory allocation.
- **Logs**: Capture detailed logs for performance issues.
- **Layout**: Analyze layout render times.

6. Common Performance Optimization Tips

- **Avoid Anonymous Functions**: Use useCallback or class methods to prevent unnecessary re-renders:

javascript

```
const onPress = useCallback(() => console.log('Button pressed'), []);
```

- **Minimize Third-Party Dependencies**: Each dependency adds overhead. Only include necessary libraries.

- **Optimize Network Requests**:

  - Use batching to reduce the number of API calls.

  - Cache frequently requested data.

- **Test on Low-End Devices**: Optimize for devices with lower processing power to ensure consistent performance.

Chapter 14: Publishing Your App

Publishing your React Native app is an exciting milestone. It involves preparing your app for production, adhering to the guidelines of the **Google Play Store** and **Apple App Store**, and establishing a robust process for managing updates and version control. This chapter will guide you through each step in detail.

---

1. Preparing Your App for Production

Before submitting your app to the app stores, it's essential to optimize and configure it for a seamless production experience.

1.1 Optimizing Your App for Release

1. **Enable Hermes (for Android):** Hermes is a lightweight JavaScript engine that improves startup times and memory usage.

    o Open android/app/build.gradle and set:

gradle

project.ext.react = [

enableHermes: true // Add this line

]

2. **Minify Code:**

   o Ensure code is minified to reduce bundle
   size:

   - **Android**: ProGuard is enabled by
     default for React Native.

   - **iOS**: Xcode automatically optimizes
     release builds.

3. **Remove Debugging Tools:**

   o Disable console logs and debugging tools in
   production:

javascript

```
if (!__DEV__) {
   console.log = () => {};
}
```

4. **Optimize Assets:**

   o Compress images and static assets.

   o Use tools like react-native-optimize-image
   to resize and optimize images.

5. **Test on Real Devices:**

- Test your app on physical devices with different screen sizes and operating system versions.

1.2 Generating Release Builds

For Android:

1. **Generate a Keystore:** Run the following command to generate a keystore:

bash

```
keytool -genkeypair -v -storetype PKCS12 -keystore my-release-key.jks -keyalg RSA -keysize 2048 -validity 10000 -alias my-key-alias
```

Save the my-release-key.jks file securely.

2. **Configure Signing:** Update android/app/build.gradle:

gradle

```
android {
  signingConfigs {
    release {
       storeFile file('my-release-key.jks')
       storePassword 'your-password'
       keyAlias 'my-key-alias'
```

```
        keyPassword 'your-key-password'

    }

}

buildTypes {

    release {

        signingConfig signingConfigs.release

    }

}

}
```

3. **Build the APK or AAB:** Build the release APK or AAB (preferred for Play Store):

bash

```
cd android
./gradlew assembleRelease   # For APK
./gradlew bundleRelease      # For AAB
```

For iOS:

1. **Configure Signing and Certificates:**
   o Open your project in Xcode (ios/<project-name>.xcworkspace).
   o Navigate to **Signing & Capabilities** and ensure a valid Apple Developer account is linked.

2. **Build the Release Version:**

   o   Archive the app: **Product > Archive**.

   o   Export the app for App Store submission.

---

2. Publishing to Google Play Store and Apple App Store

2.1 Publishing to Google Play Store

1. **Create a Developer Account:**

   o   Register at the Google Play Console with a one-time fee of $25.

2. **Create a New App:**

   o   Click **Create App**, enter app details (name, language, etc.), and choose **Free** or **Paid**.

3. **Upload Your App Bundle:**

   o   Navigate to **Production > Create Release**.

   o   Upload the AAB file (android/app/build/outputs/bundle/release/app-release.aab).

4. **Fill Store Listing Details:**

   o   Provide the app description, screenshots, feature graphic, and app icon (512x512px).

   o   Include a privacy policy URL.

5. **Submit for Review:**

- o Complete the content rating questionnaire and set app pricing.

- o Submit the app for review.

2.2 Publishing to Apple App Store

1. **Create a Developer Account:**

   - o Register at the Apple Developer Program for $99/year.

2. **Create an App in App Store Connect:**

   - o Log in to App Store Connect.

   - o Click **My Apps > New App,** and enter app details (name, bundle ID, and version).

3. **Upload the Build:**

   - o Use **Xcode** to upload your archive:

     - **Product > Archive > Distribute App**.

   - o Submit the build to App Store Connect.

4. **Fill App Information:**

   - o Provide app metadata, screenshots, and an app icon (1024x1024px).

   - o Add a privacy policy URL and define app categories.

5. **Submit for Review:**

   - o Answer the compliance questionnaire.

○ Submit the app for review.

---

3. Managing Updates and Version Control

Regular updates are essential for fixing bugs, improving performance, and adding new features.

3.1 Semantic Versioning

Follow semantic versioning (MAJOR.MINOR.PATCH):

- **Major**: Breaking changes (e.g., 2.0.0).

- **Minor**: Backward-compatible feature additions (e.g., 1.1.0).

- **Patch**: Bug fixes or performance improvements (e.g., 1.0.1).

Update the version number in:

- **Android**: android/app/build.gradle:

gradle

versionCode 2

versionName "1.1.0"

- **iOS**: ios/<project-name>/Info.plist:

xml

```
<key>CFBundleShortVersionString</key>
<string>1.1.0</string>
<key>CFBundleVersion</key>
<string>2</string>
```

3.2 Handling Over-the-Air (OTA) Updates

OTA updates allow you to deliver JavaScript changes without re-submitting to the app stores.

Using Expo Updates:

1. Install the Expo Updates library:

bash

```
npm install expo-updates
```

2. Publish updates:

bash

```
expo publish
```

Using CodePush:

1. Install react-native-code-push:

bash

```
npm install react-native-code-push
```

2. Configure your app for CodePush:

   o   Android: Add the CodePush plugin to
       MainApplication.java.

   o   iOS: Add CodePush to AppDelegate.m.

3. Push updates:

bash

```
code-push release-react <app-name> android
```

3.3 Automating Version Control with Git

Use Git for managing app versions and collaboration.

Best Practices:

- Maintain a **main** branch for stable releases.
- Use feature branches (feature/login) for new features.
- Tag releases (git tag -a v1.1.0 -m "Release v1.1.0").

Example: Git Workflow

bash

```
# Create a new feature branch
git checkout -b feature/new-feature
```

```
# Merge changes to main

git checkout main

git merge feature/new-feature


# Tag the release

git tag -a v1.1.0 -m "Release v1.1.0"


# Push changes and tags

git push origin main

git push origin –tags
```

Chapter 15: Building a Real-World App

Building a real-world app is the culmination of everything we've learned so far. In this chapter, we'll create a feature-rich **e-commerce platform** as a step-by-step guide. This project will emphasize **modular architecture**, **scalability**, and **maintainability**, incorporating best practices to ensure a professional-grade application.

1. Project Overview

The e-commerce app will include:

1. A **Product List**: Displaying available products.

2. A **Product Detail** page: Showing detailed information and allowing the user to add items to a cart.

3. A **Cart**: Allowing users to view selected items and proceed to checkout.

4. **User Authentication**: Providing login and signup functionality.

5. **Scalability**: Organized components, reusable modules, and proper state management.

Technologies Used:

- React Native for UI development.

- Context API for global state management.

- react-navigation for navigation.

- axios for API integration.

- react-native-fast-image for optimized image handling.

---

2. Setting Up the Project

2.1 Initializing the Project

Start a new React Native project:

bash

npx react-native init ECommerceApp

cd ECommerceApp

npm install @react-navigation/native react-navigation-stack react-native-screens react-native-safe-area-context react-native-gesture-handler react-native-reanimated react-native-vector-icons axios react-native-fast-image

2.2 Folder Structure

Organize the app into a scalable folder structure:

graphql

```
ECommerceApp/
├── src/
│   ├── components/     # Reusable UI components
│   ├── screens/        # Individual screens (Home, ProductDetail, Cart, etc.)
│   ├── context/        # Global state management
│   ├── navigation/     # Navigation configurations
│   ├── services/       # API and utility functions
│   ├── assets/         # Images, fonts, etc.
│   ├── styles/         # Global styles
```

```
|   ├── App.js        # Entry point
```

---

3. Building Core Features

3.1 Product List

Goal: Display a list of products fetched from an API.

Step 1: API Service Create a service function in src/services/api.js:

javascript

```javascript
import axios from 'axios';


const API_BASE_URL = 'https://fakestoreapi.com';


export const getProducts = async () => {
  try {
    const response = await axios.get(`${API_BASE_URL}/products`);
    return response.data;
  } catch (error) {
    console.error('Error fetching products:', error);
    throw error;
```

```
    }
};
```

Step 2: Product List Screen Create
src/screens/ProductList.js:

javascript

```javascript
import React, { useEffect, useState } from 'react';
import { View, Text, FlatList, StyleSheet,
TouchableOpacity } from 'react-native';
import FastImage from 'react-native-fast-image';
import { getProducts } from '../services/api';

const ProductList = ({ navigation }) => {
  const [products, setProducts] = useState([]);

  useEffect(() => {
    const fetchProducts = async () => {
      const data = await getProducts();
      setProducts(data);
    };

    fetchProducts();
  }, []);
```

```
  return (
    <FlatList
      data={products}
      keyExtractor={(item) => item.id.toString()}
      renderItem={({ item }) => (
        <TouchableOpacity
          onPress={() =>
navigation.navigate('ProductDetail', { product: item })}
          >
            <View style={styles.item}>
              <FastImage style={styles.image} source={{
uri: item.image }} />
              <Text
style={styles.title}>{item.title}</Text>
              <Text
style={styles.price}>${item.price}</Text>
            </View>
          </TouchableOpacity>
        )}
      />
    );
  };
```

```
const styles = StyleSheet.create({
    item: {
        flexDirection: 'row',
        padding: 10,
        borderBottomWidth: 1,
        borderBottomColor: '#ccc',
    },
    image: {
        width: 50,
        height: 50,
        marginRight: 10,
    },
    title: {
        fontSize: 16,
        flex: 1,
    },
    price: {
        fontSize: 16,
        fontWeight: 'bold',
    },
});
```

```javascript
export default ProductList;
```

3.2 Product Detail

Goal: Display detailed information about a product and allow adding it to the cart.

Create src/screens/ProductDetail.js:

javascript

```javascript
import React, { useContext } from 'react';
import { View, Text, StyleSheet, Button } from 'react-native';
import FastImage from 'react-native-fast-image';
import { CartContext } from '../context/CartContext';

const ProductDetail = ({ route }) => {
    const { product } = route.params;
    const { addToCart } = useContext(CartContext);

    return (
        <View style={styles.container}>
            <FastImage style={styles.image} source={{ uri: product.image }} />
```

```jsx
      <Text style={styles.title}>{product.title}</Text>
      <Text
style={styles.price}>${product.price}</Text>
      <Text
style={styles.description}>{product.description}</Text>
      <Button title="Add to Cart" onPress={() =>
addToCart(product)} />
    </View>
  );
};


const styles = StyleSheet.create({
  container: {
    padding: 20,
  },
  image: {
    width: '100%',
    height: 200,
  },
  title: {
    fontSize: 24,
    fontWeight: 'bold',
    marginVertical: 10,
```

```
  },
  price: {
    fontSize: 20,
    color: 'green',
    marginVertical: 10,
  },
  description: {
    fontSize: 16,
    marginVertical: 10,
  },
});
```

export default ProductDetail;

3.3 Cart

Goal: Show a list of selected items and their total price.

Step 1: Create Cart Context Create
src/context/CartContext.js:

javascript

```
import React, { createContext, useState } from 'react';
```

```javascript
export const CartContext = createContext();

export const CartProvider = ({ children }) => {
  const [cart, setCart] = useState([]);

  const addToCart = (product) => {
    setCart((prevCart) => [...prevCart, product]);
  };

  const removeFromCart = (id) => {
    setCart((prevCart) => prevCart.filter((item) => item.id !== id));
  };

  return (
    <CartContext.Provider value={{ cart, addToCart, removeFromCart }}>
      {children}
    </CartContext.Provider>
  );
};
```

Wrap the app in CartProvider:

javascript

```javascript
import { CartProvider } from './src/context/CartContext';

const App = () => (
  <CartProvider>
    <Navigation />
  </CartProvider>
);

export default App;
```

Step 2: Create Cart Screen Create src/screens/Cart.js:

javascript

```javascript
import React, { useContext } from 'react';
import { View, Text, FlatList, StyleSheet, Button } from 'react-native';
import { CartContext } from '../context/CartContext';

const Cart = () => {
  const { cart, removeFromCart } = useContext(CartContext);
```

```jsx
  const total = cart.reduce((sum, item) => sum +
item.price, 0);


  return (
    <View style={styles.container}>
      <FlatList
        data={cart}
        keyExtractor={(item) => item.id.toString()}
        renderItem={({ item }) => (
          <View style={styles.item}>
            <Text>{item.title}</Text>
            <Text>${item.price}</Text>
            <Button title="Remove" onPress={() =>
removeFromCart(item.id)} />
          </View>
        )}
      />
      <Text style={styles.total}>Total:
${total.toFixed(2)}</Text>
    </View>
  );
};
```

```javascript
const styles = StyleSheet.create({
  container: {
    padding: 20,
  },
  item: {
    flexDirection: 'row',
    justifyContent: 'space-between',
    marginVertical: 10,
  },
  total: {
    fontSize: 18,
    fontWeight: 'bold',
    marginTop: 20,
  },
});

export default Cart;
```

4. Modular Architecture, Scalability, and Maintainability

4.1 Modular Architecture

- **Separation of Concerns**: Divide your app into components, screens, services, and context for better maintainability.

- **Reusable Components**: Extract commonly used UI elements (e.g., buttons, headers) into src/components.

4.2 Scalability

- **Dynamic API Integration**: Use a central configuration file for API URLs.

- **State Management**: Start with Context API, and move to Redux for complex apps.

- **Lazy Loading**: Use dynamic imports to load heavy screens only when needed.

4.3 Maintainability

- **Type Safety**: Use TypeScript to enforce type safety and reduce runtime errors.

- **Code Reviews**: Implement a code review process to maintain high standards.

- **Testing**: Add unit tests for critical components and API integration.

Chapter 16: React Native for Teams

Building and maintaining large-scale React Native projects often involves multiple developers working collaboratively. Effective workflows, collaboration tools, and best practices are essential for ensuring high code quality, smooth development, and scalable applications. This chapter focuses on managing React Native projects in a team environment, emphasizing tools for collaboration, code quality, pull requests, and large-scale app management.

---

1. Collaboration Tools and Workflows

Collaboration in React Native projects requires tools that streamline communication, version control, and task management. Here are the key components of a collaborative workflow:

1.1 Version Control with Git

Git is the backbone of collaborative development, allowing teams to manage changes and collaborate on the same codebase.

Best Practices for Git in Teams:

- **Branching Strategy**:

- Use a structured branching model like GitFlow:
  - **main**: Stable, production-ready code.
  - **develop**: Features under development.
  - **feature/**: Individual feature branches.
- Example workflow:

bash

```
# Create a feature branch
git checkout -b feature/login
```

```
# Push changes to remote
git push origin feature/login
```

```
# Merge to develop after review
git checkout develop
git merge feature/login
```

- **Commit Messages**:
  - Use clear, descriptive commit messages:

plaintext

feat: Add login functionality

fix: Resolve image loading bug

refactor: Simplify product list rendering

- **Code Reviews**:
    - Enforce pull requests (PRs) for merging code into main or develop.
    - Use tools like GitHub, GitLab, or Bitbucket for reviewing PRs.

1.2 Task Management

Effective task management ensures that all team members are aligned on project goals.

Recommended Tools:

- **Jira**: Comprehensive tool for agile workflows, including sprint planning.
- **Trello**: Kanban-style boards for managing tasks visually.
- **Notion**: Flexible for documentation and task tracking.

Best Practices:

- Break tasks into smaller units (e.g., "Implement login screen UI").
- Use labels or tags to indicate task priority and status.

1.3 Communication Tools

Seamless communication is critical for resolving blockers and sharing updates.

Popular Communication Tools:

- **Slack**: Great for real-time communication.
- **Microsoft Teams**: Includes video calls and integrations with task management tools.
- **Zoom**: Reliable for remote team meetings.

Best Practices:

- Create dedicated channels for features or components (e.g., #authentication, #navigation).
- Schedule daily standups to track progress.

---

2. Code Quality

High-quality code is essential for maintainability, scalability, and performance. Here's how teams can enforce quality standards:

2.1 Code Reviews and Pull Requests

Pull requests (PRs) ensure that every change is reviewed before merging into the main codebase.

Best Practices for Pull Requests:

- **Small PRs**:

- o Keep PRs focused on a single feature or fix to simplify reviews.

- **Clear Descriptions**:
  - o Include a summary of the changes and testing instructions:

markdown

Summary

- Added login screen UI

- Integrated with API for authentication

Testing

- Log in with valid credentials

- Ensure error messages are displayed for invalid credentials

- **Peer Reviews**:
  - o At least one team member should review the code before merging.

- **Automated Checks**:
  - o Use CI/CD pipelines to run tests and linters on every PR.

2.2 Code Formatting and Linting

Consistent code formatting improves readability and reduces errors.

Tools for Code Formatting:

- **Prettier**: Automatically formats code to a consistent style.

bash

```bash
npm install --save-dev prettier
```

Setting Up Prettier:

- Add a .prettierrc file:

json

```json
{
  "singleQuote": true,
  "trailingComma": "all"
}
```

Linting with ESLint:

- ESLint helps identify and fix common coding errors.

bash

```bash
npm install --save-dev eslint
npx eslint --init
```

Best Practices:

- Combine Prettier with ESLint for both formatting and linting:

bash

```
npm install --save-dev eslint-config-prettier eslint-plugin-prettier
```

- Enforce formatting in the development workflow:
  - Use Git hooks with husky to lint and format code before committing:

bash

```
npm install --save-dev husky lint-staged
npx husky add .husky/pre-commit "npx lint-staged"
```

2.3 Writing Tests

Automated tests catch issues early and improve confidence in code changes.

Types of Tests:

1. **Unit Tests**:
   - Test individual functions or components.
   - Use Jest and React Testing Library.

bash

```
npm install --save-dev jest @testing-library/react-native
```

2. **Integration Tests**:

   o Test interactions between components.

   o Simulate navigation or API calls.

3. **End-to-End Tests**:

   o Validate the entire user flow using tools like Detox or Appium.

Best Practices:

- Aim for a mix of test types (e.g., 70% unit, 20% integration, 10% end-to-end).

- Automate test execution in the CI pipeline.

---

3. Managing Large-Scale Apps

Large-scale React Native projects require scalable architectures and robust processes to maintain quality as the team and codebase grow.

3.1 Modular Architecture

Divide the app into logical modules or features to reduce complexity.

Example Folder Structure:

bash

```
src/
├── features/          # Feature-based modules
│   ├── authentication/
│   │   ├── components/
│   │   ├── screens/
│   │   └── context/
│   ├── cart/
│   │   ├── components/
│   │   ├── screens/
│   │   └── context/
│   └── products/
│       ├── components/
│       ├── screens/
│       └── context/
├── shared/            # Reusable components and utilities
│   ├── components/
│   ├── hooks/
│   ├── styles/
│   └── utils/
```

3.2 State Management

Choose a state management approach that suits your app's complexity:

- **Small-Scale Apps**:
    - o Use the Context API for global state (e.g., user authentication, cart).

- **Large-Scale Apps**:
    - o Use Redux for predictable state updates.

bash

npm install redux react-redux @reduxjs/toolkit

Best Practices:

- Keep state slices small and modular.

- Use middleware like Redux Thunk for async actions.

3.3 Performance Optimization

Large-scale apps must maintain performance across a growing codebase.

Key Strategies:

- **Optimize Rendering**:
    - o Use React.memo for components that don't need frequent updates.

- **Lazy Load Features**:

- o Dynamically load screens to reduce initial load time:

javascript

```javascript
const ProductDetail = React.lazy(() =>
import('./screens/ProductDetail'));
```

- **Avoid Memory Leaks**:
  - o Clean up timers, listeners, and API calls in useEffect cleanup functions.

3.4 Documentation

Documenting processes and code ensures that new team members can onboard quickly.

Recommended Documentation Tools:

- **Confluence**: Centralized knowledge base for teams.

- **Notion**: Flexible for project documentation.

- **Storybook**: Interactive UI documentation for React Native components.

---

4. Continuous Integration and Deployment

Automating testing and deployment ensures consistent quality across all team contributions.

4.1 Setting Up CI/CD

Tools:

- **GitHub Actions**: Free for small projects.
- **CircleCI**: Great for large teams and parallel builds.
- **Bitrise**: Tailored for mobile apps.

Example CI Workflow (GitHub Actions):

yaml

```
name: React Native CI

on:
  push:
    branches:
      - main
  pull_request:
    branches:
      - main

jobs:
  test:
    runs-on: ubuntu-latest
```

```
steps:

  - name: Checkout code

    uses: actions/checkout@v3


  - name: Set up Node.js

    uses: actions/setup-node@v3

    with:

      node-version: 16


  - name: Install dependencies

    run: npm install


  - name: Run tests

    run: npm test
```

4.2 Automating App Deployment

Android:

- Use Gradle commands to build and upload the app to the Play Store.

iOS:

- Automate builds and submissions to the App Store using Fastlane:

bash

```
npm install -g fastlane
fastlane init
fastlane deliver
```

Chapter 17: The Future of React Native

As a leading framework for cross-platform mobile app development, React Native has undergone significant evolution since its inception in 2015. This chapter explores **React Native's roadmap**, the **evolving ecosystem**, and how React Native compares to its **alternatives**. We'll also discuss where React Native stands in the fast-changing tech landscape and its potential for the future.

---

1. React Native's Roadmap and Evolving Ecosystem

1.1 React Native's Current State

React Native allows developers to write mobile applications for **iOS** and **Android** using JavaScript and React. Key features include:

- **Code Reusability**: Write once, deploy across platforms.

- **Rich Ecosystem**: Access to thousands of libraries and plugins.

- **Active Community**: Supported by Facebook (now Meta) and an open-source community.

1.2 Key Roadmap Highlights

React Native's future focuses on enhancing **performance**, **developer experience**, and **platform parity**.

1. **Fabric Renderer**:

   o **What is it?** Fabric is React Native's new rendering engine, designed to unify the rendering pipeline and improve performance.

   o **Key Benefits**:

      ▪ Synchronization between React and native views for smoother animations.

      ▪ Support for incremental rendering for faster UI updates.

   o **Status**: Fabric is being gradually integrated into React Native.

2. **Turbo Modules**:

   o **What is it?** Turbo Modules replace the older native module system, providing faster initialization and better memory management.

   o **Key Features**:

      ▪ Lazily loaded modules, reducing startup times.

      ▪ Enhanced performance for apps using multiple native modules.

- o **Status**: Already available and being adopted by developers.

3. **Codegen**:

    - o **What is it?** A tool to generate type-safe, native code automatically for native modules.

    - o **Key Benefits**:

        - Reduces boilerplate code for bridging native modules.

        - Increases reliability through type safety.

4. **Multi-Platform Support**:

    - o React Native is expanding its capabilities beyond iOS and Android:

        - **Windows**: React Native for Windows is already in use for desktop apps.

        - **macOS**: React Native for macOS extends its use for Apple desktops.

        - **Web**: React Native Web brings React Native components to browsers.

1.3 Trends in the React Native Ecosystem

1. **Deeper Integration with JavaScript Frameworks**:

- o Frameworks like **Next.js** and **Expo** are enhancing React Native's capabilities for web and mobile development.

2. **Focus on Performance**:

- o Community-driven libraries like react-native-reanimated and react-native-gesture-handler are becoming staples for creating smooth animations and interactions.

3. **Developer Experience**:

- o Tools like Flipper, Expo's development tools, and enhancements in Metro bundler make debugging and profiling easier.

4. **Cross-Platform UI Libraries**:

- o Libraries like **React Native Paper** and **React Native Elements** are maturing, allowing faster development of cohesive UI across platforms.

---

2. Alternatives to React Native

While React Native is a dominant force in cross-platform development, several alternatives cater to specific needs. Here's a comparison of React Native and its competitors.

2.1 Flutter

Overview:

- Created by Google, Flutter uses the Dart language to build cross-platform apps.

Strengths:

- **Performance**: Flutter apps are compiled into native machine code, resulting in excellent performance.
- **Widget System**: Provides a rich set of customizable widgets.
- **Hot Reload**: Like React Native, Flutter offers fast iteration through hot reload.
- **Unified Codebase**: Flutter supports web, desktop, and mobile from a single codebase.

Weaknesses:

- **Learning Curve**: Dart is less familiar to developers compared to JavaScript.
- **App Size**: Flutter apps tend to be larger than React Native apps.

React Native vs. Flutter:

Feature	React Native	Flutter
Language	JavaScript/TypeScript	Dart
Performance	Good, with optimizations	Excellent (native code)
Community Support	Larger, older community	Growing rapidly
UI Customization	Relies on native views	Fully customizable UI

2.2 Kotlin Multiplatform Mobile (KMM)

Overview:

- Kotlin Multiplatform allows sharing code between Android and iOS while writing platform-specific UIs.

Strengths:

- **Platform-Specific APIs**: Full access to native features of Android and iOS.

- **Performance**: Native performance due to platform-specific UIs.

- **Compatibility**: Integrates seamlessly with existing native codebases.

Weaknesses:

- **Limited Sharing**: Only the business logic is shared, not the UI.

- **Steeper Learning Curve**: Requires knowledge of native development for UI layers.

React Native vs. KMM:

Feature	React Native	KMM
Code Reuse	High (UI and logic)	Moderate (logic only)
Performance	Good	Excellent
Community	Larger	Smaller, growing

Feature	React Native	KMM
Support		

2.3 Xamarin

Overview:

- Xamarin, backed by Microsoft, uses C# for cross-platform development.

Strengths:

- **Native Performance**: Uses native bindings for high performance.

- **Integration**: Seamless integration with Microsoft's ecosystem (e.g., Azure).

Weaknesses:

- **Tooling**: Slower development process compared to React Native or Flutter.

- **App Size**: Larger binaries compared to React Native.

React Native vs. Xamarin:

Feature	React Native	Xamarin
Language	JavaScript/TypeScript	C#
Performance	Good	Good
Ease of Use	Easier to learn	Harder for non-C# devs

2.4 SwiftUI and Jetpack Compose

Overview:

- **SwiftUI**: Apple's framework for declarative UI on iOS/macOS.

- **Jetpack Compose**: Google's framework for declarative UI on Android.

Strengths:

- **Native Development**: Best for platform-specific features.

- **Performance**: Superior native performance.

- **Modern Frameworks**: Simplified, declarative approach to UI.

Weaknesses:

- **Single Platform**: No cross-platform support.

React Native vs. SwiftUI/Jetpack Compose:

Feature	React Native	SwiftUI/Jetpack Compose
Cross-Platform	Yes	No
Performance	Good	Excellent
Learning Curve	Moderate	Steep

3. The Future of React Native

3.1 Key Advantages of React Native

1. **JavaScript Ecosystem**:

   - Leverages JavaScript, the most popular programming language, ensuring a steady influx of developers.

2. **Community Support**:

   - A massive open-source community ensures continued growth, updates, and support.

3. **Meta's Commitment**:

   - As the creator and maintainer, Meta (Facebook) uses React Native for its own apps, ensuring long-term investment.

4. **Growing Flexibility**:

   - Expanding support for platforms like web, Windows, and macOS makes React Native a versatile tool for cross-platform needs.

3.2 Challenges for React Native

1. **Performance Bottlenecks**:

   - Despite improvements, React Native still faces challenges in rendering complex animations and managing large datasets.

2. **Competition**:

o Frameworks like Flutter and SwiftUI are gaining traction due to their unique strengths.

3. **Tooling Gaps**:

   o Some areas, like debugging native modules or profiling complex performance issues, still lack mature tooling.

3.3 Predictions for React Native's Future

1. **Convergence of Platforms**:

   o React Native's focus on expanding to desktop and web platforms positions it as a unified development framework.

2. **Increased Enterprise Adoption**:

   o Companies like Microsoft (using React Native for Windows) signal growing adoption in the enterprise world.

3. **Enhanced Performance**:

   o Features like Fabric and Turbo Modules will address key performance concerns, making React Native suitable for more demanding applications.

4. **AI and AR/VR Support**:

- o With frameworks like TensorFlow.js and ARKit integrations, React Native may play a role in emerging AI and AR/VR applications.

Conclusion

React Native's flexibility, robust community, and continuous evolution make it a strong contender for cross-platform development in the coming years. While alternatives like Flutter and KMM offer compelling advantages, React Native's widespread adoption and focus on improving performance and developer experience ensure its relevance in the rapidly changing mobile app ecosystem. As we look ahead, React Native's commitment to unifying platforms and addressing developer pain points suggests it will remain a cornerstone of cross-platform development for years to come.

www.ingramcontent.com/pod-product-compliance
Lightning Source LLC
LaVergne TN
LVHW051322050326
832903LV00031B/3312